HBCUNOMICS:

A STORY OF THE POWER OF BLACK COLLEGE STUDENTS, ECONOMIC SELF-SUFFICIENCY AND FINANCIAL FREEDOM

"finally a fictional financial
education book for our culture"

by

Jamerus Payton

Published by
The Payton Publishing Group, LLC
Copyright © 2020 by Jamerus Payton
First Edition

ISBN: 978-1-7342810-0-2

Manufactured in USA
For information about custom editions, special sales,
premium and corporate purchases, please contact
jamerus@jameruspayton.com.
Printed by 48HrBooks.com

"Conquering a pre-existing mindset
is worth more than millions. In fact, more times
than not, those millions that you seek are on
the other side of that defeat."
-Jamerus Payton

CONTENTS

DEDICATION

This book is dedicated to my Granddad, Tedock Bell, who was fatally shot in 1967 during the Newark Riots by a police officer. It is 2020, and these occurrences are still happening. This creative work of art is an example of how to turn tragedy into an actionable solution.

This book is also dedicated to my family. I have left you all a blueprint to build legacies and fortunes. If you do not remember anything else that I have taught you, please remember that: "Your time here is limited. Spread the genius that's in your heart and mind while you can."

ACKNOWLEDGMENTS

Special thanks are given to The Most High God, to myself, my <u>real</u> family, <u>real</u> friends, <u>real</u> business partners, <u>real</u> mentors and community for believing. A lot of people and experiences helped with the creation of this book. Without my village and tribe, I wouldn't have been able to complete this project. Thank you for understanding, trusting and putting up with a guy from Greenville, North Carolina and his vision.

FOREWORD

WRITTEN BY
ASH CASH EVANTUS

When Jay-Z said that financial freedom was our only hope, he was not exaggerating. We now live in a world where it is more than evident that if you want justice, freedom and the pursuit of happiness, then economics aka financial freedom is the way to make that happen.

Unfortunately, financial education in our community isn't taught at an early age and, because a lot of us are not given stories of economic empowerment at home, we become adults, learning to fend for ourselves.

My brother, Jamerus Payton, has been on the forefront of helping the culture move forward economically for many years. As the Owner of The Payton Insurance Group, LLC and Cofounder of HBCU Wall Street, which are both helping Black families, businesses, and investors educate and sustain themselves, I was excited when I heard that this book was being written.

Just to give some context, HBCUs are an important part of our financial freedom. I once saw a post that said that HBCUs are responsible for:

75% of Black PhDs
46% of Black business executives
50% of Black Engineers
80% of Black federal judges
85% of Black doctors
50% of Black attorneys
75% of Black military officers
40% of Black dentists
50% of Black pharmacists
75% of Black veterinarians

With those types of numbers HBCUs are vital to our financial freedom, and HBCUNomics is a great way to marry the power of HBCUs with the financial knowledge that many of us are missing. HBCUNomics will teach readers how to practice healthy capitalism in our community to make sure that we are buying back our blocks so that we are rebuilding the Black Wall Streets.

The truth of the matter is that money is power! Those who control the money, control everything else... Politics, Schools, Business, Police, Community and everything else in between.

Many believe that the racial injustices that many Blacks face in America (and around the world) boils down to simply hating someone for the color of their skin and that simply having other ethnicities be more sympathetic to our plight would make things better... I disagree.

Just to be clear, racism isn't what the dictionary and the media want you to believe it is - which is defined as prejudice, discrimination, or antagonism directed against someone of a different race based on the belief that one's own race is superior.

The true definition of racism (as stated by Dr. Claude Anderson in his powerful book #Powernomics) is when one group holds a disproportionate share of wealth and power over another group then uses those resources to marginalize, exploit, exclude and subordinate the weaker group. That's why when you turn on the television it seems like African-Americans are losing every-day! Because of systemic and institutionalized racism!

Without getting too deep into the history of Black economics, we must realize that most Blacks have only been able to create 'real' wealth and financial freedom for the last 50 years – slavery lasted 223 years from 1640-1863, then reconstruction and Jim Crow laws lasted 102 years from 1863-1965. It wasn't until the post-civil rights era that we began to see the tides change. And to be clear, most of this was LEGAL and sanctioned by the government.

This is why HBCUNomics is important. If we want to change our socioeconomic conditions and create true and lasting wealth, we do not have to look any further than within our own communities and our own institutions. HBCUs are the epicenter for economic development in the Black community, and HBCUNomics will give you the tips, tools and resources to make that a reality. It's time for us to write our OWN stories! As the late great Malcom X once stated, "Only a fool will let his enemy educate his children."

THE PERFECT DAY

I t's my first day of retirement, and my alarm still goes off at 5:45 am. I reach over dazed and confused as I've done every morning since I first got the alarm clock back in college. As I turn on my lamp, I can't help but to focus my eyes on the words:

"Our lives should be lived not avoiding problems but welcoming them as challenges that will strengthen us so we can be victorious in the future. When you know The Most High, there is nothing to fear."

Those were my Grandma Lindsey's parting words. They now sit nestled under the large framed picture of my Grandparents and I on the football field during homecoming. It was a picture given to me on my 18th birthday. Because of these words, I'm a man with little worries in life. Those words shaped every decision I made after she left us. Every new business venture I started, those words stuck with me. My business deals, real estate deals, my generosity - none of those would have been mine if I had not taken heed of the words of my Grandma Lindsey.

Over the years, getting out of bed hasn't been the struggle that it once was. It turns out, I am actually a morning person after all. Life has a funny way of revealing its true self when you're aligned with your passion and purpose.

I immediately head to the bathroom to brush my teeth, wash my face, and put on my favorite orange alma mater t-shirt as I get ready to walk to the beach before sunrise.

I still can't believe the lessons from my grandparents and years of planting financial seeds have finally created the life that I dreamt of when I first stepped onto the campus of my alma mater, Earl Graves College (EGC). As I turn off the electric toothbrush, my eyes are fixated on "The Lord's Prayer (The Law Of Attraction Version)" taped to my mirror. Before leaving the house, I stop by the left side of the bed to kiss my wife Rachel's warm forehead as she snores abruptly. For the first time in a long time, I'm drawn in by her tattoo. It is a tattoo that we both got on our honeymoon, "Dream big or stay in bed." I instantly chuckle at the irony. Not because she's still in bed but because, together, we have amassed a great fortune and rest is something she deserves at this point. We have poured into each other since that first real estate deal back in college. And now, watching her sleep peacefully, all I can think is "she's still up to something, she's still going."

After 50 years, she still doesn't believe me when I tell her that she snores, it's crazy! Her once thick jet black hair is now a perfectly grayed color. It's beautiful, and til this day, she's still beautiful in her sleep. I almost cry thinking about the financial sacrifices that we both had to make over the years, but our current lifestyle shows though not easy or fair, it was worth it. As I walk down our oakwood stairs I can already smell the fresh aroma of Tanzanian Peaberry Coffee in the air from the coffee machine. It's by far the best coffee brand in Africa; I'd even say in the world. Grown on Mount Meru and Mount Kilimanjaro, it's the perfect blend of amazingness.

I look at the clock, 6:15 A.M.. I only have 8 minutes before watching the beautiful Ada Beach sunrise in Ada, Ghana. I grab my coffee, a bowl of fruit that I had prepped the night before, and the local Sunday newspaper off the doorstep. I grab my book and my laptop and rush out the door.

Today, I decide to walk to the beach without shoes. There's something about the sand biting the bottom of my feet that reminds me I am in God's country. As I walk over the white sand dunes, the view is breathtaking. Though I've been doing this routine for the last 30 days now, it never ceases to amaze me, nor does it get old. The clear blue water marries itself to the white sand. The sky is an orange-red color filled with rare sea birds, it's a sight to behold.

As I sit on the beach, I check my phone and see multiple unread emails. I contemplate for a moment whether I should open them. The first email is from my alma mater. I almost can't believe it! They want to retire my basketball jersey, number twelve, and dedicate the new School of Business to me! Over the years, our Bell

Family Foundation has given back a substantial amount of money to the once struggling endowment. I immediately email back agreeing and letting them know that it MUST have my wife's name on it as well. I think to myself, "The Jah-Regal and Rachel Bell School Of Business." It has a nice ring to it. Rachel is going to be ecstatic to hear this surprising news!

After the first email, I check to see what other great news may be waiting for me. The next email is from my Certified Public Accountant (CPA), James McCarthy. It shows me the financial statement from all the businesses that we spent years vertically integrating. It was always our goal to control the entire supply chain and value systems for our operations. According to the email, it looks like we are definitely doing just that and doing it well might I add. His email simply reads,"

"Great decision to license your company's logo to that apparel company. That additional income should really help with this quarter's numbers. - J. Mac"

The next email is from my daughter. I am so proud of her. She's now the Chief Executive Officer (CEO) of our Family Food Enterprise. As a family, we turned a single food venture that I started back in college into a billion dollar food franchise empire. Since taking over the business, her strategies have built shareholder confidence to an all time high. She is emailing me to check in. She does that from time to time. She always wanted me to let her run the company the way she wanted to, and she is doing very well. Every now and then though, she reaches out to see what I think when she is going to implement a new strategy, or to tell me some good news. It feels good to see we have successfully raised our children to become the version of success they desired... a version we are extremely proud of.

As I'm just about to put my phone down to watch the sunrise, an email from my youngest son pops in. He is now the Senior Vice President (SVP) of our family's real estate company. He asks if I have any advice before closing on the new land deal for our expansion in Ghana. I simply tell him what my Dad once told me, "*Do the stuff that works and stop doing the stuff that does not. I trust you and I love you!*" Collectively, we've been preparing your entire life for this moment." As I'm typing, I'm reminded of the line from the movie "Black Panther":

"A man that has not prepared his own children for his death has failed as a father." -King T'Chaka

Though I'm not going anywhere anytime soon, it is something that every parent and grandparent wonders and hopes for.

I am so thankful that my Grandma so many years ago thought beyond her life. She planted the seed of her legacy and trusted me to turn the $250,000 life insurance inheritance she left in my name into the Bell family fortune. I'm sure she would be proud of the progress we have made since that day. I could have never imagined the plans and ideas I came up with as a college student would one day be worth more than $200 billion. But our family has done it. Sitting here on this beach, at this moment, I can't help but smile at the accomplishment. No other family business has been able to amass what we have since Sam Walton's Family Empire.

The last email that I check is from my oldest son, he is the Founder and Managing Partner of our family equity firm. It is the leading private equity firm focused on investing and driving value creation in technology, telecommunications, and food science companies. He is excited to have found a handful of companies founded by HBCU graduates to invest in. His email reads:

"Old Man,

Hope you're enjoying retirement! I can't believe you actually did it!

Really quickly though, when you get a chance I would like to get your thoughts on 3 startup companies that are founded by some high potential HBCU students and alumni. They are really on to some big things, Dad! I mean game-changing technology that will really help them push families, communities and the culture forward. With our team's resources and capital, I think they would do really well in their respective markets, especially the Space-focused startup company. They are working on commercial-use technologies, products and services for Space in transportation, energy, entertainment, construction and hospitality. With the commercial space market recently becoming a $4.2 trillion dollar industry, I think there's

even some initial public offering (IPO)
potential with this one!
    Anyway, let's talk soon!
    I Love You and Congrats on retirement.
You truly deserve it!
    P.S. - Now that you're retired, maybe we
can get Mom to finally join you! :)"

As the sun begins to rise over the ocean, a large tear of joy begins to roll down my cheek. "Fulfillment and faithfulness." They are the only words that could describe my perfect life in this perfect full circle moment.

As if scripted, my wife Rachel touches my shoulder....I'm slightly startled but don't show it. As I look up, I hear her angelic and calming voice, "Hey, Food Truck Genius!" It was a name given to me by her many moons ago. "I decided to join you this morning, and I have some great news. You were already sound asleep last night, so I didn't want to wake you, but I DID IT! I closed my largest commercial real estate deal to date last night! I finally purchased a small abandoned town! I finally got it!"

"WOW!! I knew it! I knew you were up to something, but this *far* exceeds what I thought you were working on. You still never cease to amaze me, Queen!" We both smile at one another. I reach up to my shoulder and gently squeeze her small pecan tan colored hand.

"Well, I have some great news too, Rachel! EGC decided to name the new School of Business building after us. It's going to be named, "The Jah-Regal and Rachel Bell School Of Business"

"That's AMAZING news, Jah! I'm so proud of you!" She exclaimed.

I immediately corrected her by saying "No, I'm proud of us!" As the sunrise continues to gleam over the calm water, we both admire its beauty. If I know my wife, and I do, she is thinking the same thing as me. We sit, silently in admiration of the life that two Black kids with Black college education have built. This is shaping up to be the perfect day!

THE DECISION

DOWNTOWN NEWARK

The morning sun shone through my window, the rays kissing my face as I woke up. The scent of chicken, waffles, homemade donuts, eggs, bacon, and grits filled the air. I could hear the sounds of Thelonius Monk and John Coltrane playing from the kitchen. It could only mean one thing, it is my birthday. Not just any birthday, it is my 18th birthday today. This birthday breakfast tradition was started by my Dad many years ago. The smile on my face soon wore off as I set my eyes on my Dad's picture. A tear immediately streamed down my cheek. This would be the second consecutive year I would be celebrating my birthday without him. He's not in prison nor did my parents divorce. He passed away three days after my 16th birthday. Life hasn't been as fun without him, but I keep moving forward. We immediately went from a comfortable middle class lifestyle to a low income black family in a matter of months. Since then, my Mom, a teacher, had to work three jobs to put food on the table.

CHAPTER ONE

I am Jah-Regal Bell, but most of my friends, family, and teammates call me "Jah." I am a Senior at Septima Clark High School and a left-handed 6'8 star shooting guard for the basketball team. I'm most proud of the fact that in addition to being an All-American on the basketball court, I am also a high school All-American in the classroom with a 3.8 GPA.

I dried off my face as Mom told me Grandma Lindsey has a surprise gift for me. She always did. After this year's season opener, she got me a retro Magic Johnson jersey, matching sneakers and some stocks for scoring over 2,000 points in my high basketball career. For New Jersey High School boys basketball, this is a great honor.

Despite what I did on the court, it was always what I did in the classroom that impressed her most. Even though I had a demanding basketball schedule and dramatic family changes, she always rewarded me for my resilience to shine in the classroom. My family truly valued education and not just classroom education but applied knowledge.

"Grandma is sorry she couldn't make it today," my Mom said, "but she sends her regards and a gift."

"Can I see it now?" I asked, eager to know what Grandma Lindsey got me, but I knew what my Mom's answer would be.

"Get your butt to school boy. It's a surprise, and you'll get to open it at dinner," she said.

I got ready for school, and she offered to drop me off. Mom taught at the nearby school and tutored students in her free time. She was also a bus driver - a job she picked up after Dad's passing to bring in extra cash. A parting kiss from her, and I watched her drive off. She would never let me work. Grandma Lindsey was also against the idea; She feared losing me like she lost her son.

My Dad, Jamon, once an aspiring Mechanical Engineer from a top Black Engineering college, was a mechanic at the local auto shop. He was on the verge of establishing his trucking and trailer repair shop before passing away unexpectedly. He and my Mom met and fell in love while in college; however, once he found out that my Mom was pregnant with me, he decided to drop out to help take care of us so that my Mom could finish college. Being the first college graduate in her family was always important to her, and he made sure he helped her succeed. Despite being a mechanic, he was by far the smartest man that I knew. He would read about any and every subject. He loved music, especially jazz, blues and rock music. He would always quote Bob Marley by saying, "One good thing about music, when it hits you, you feel no pain." Life was rosy for us as he always ensured we had the best money could buy. His death severely disrupted our standard of living and life as we knew it. Despite having life insurance, he didn't have a substantial life insurance policy, so that left us struggling to survive. Like most working people, he had a group term insurance policy through his job, but it was nowhere near enough to take care of us after his death. He believed he had more time. He would mention to my Mom occasionally that he needed to and would review their policy and increase the insurance, but time ran out with his passing.

✶ ✶ ✶ ✶ ✶

While at school, I watched the clock tick away, my heart beating with every tick, tick, tick. The day was unusually slow and I couldn't wait for the closing bell to know what Grandma Lindsey got for me. This year was different. I'd turned 18 and was going off to college, so I figured the gift would be something I'd love.

"Why wouldn't it be?" That's what I asked myself. Grandma Lindsey always got me gifts I would love.

"Jah-Regal! Jah-Regal Bell!" a voice screamed my name, and I was brought back to reality. It was my teacher.

"Did you hear me? Where has your mind drifted to?"

"The National Bureau of Economic Research (NBER) announced today that we are officially in a recession. The worst since the Great Depression of the 1930s." He asked, "Can you define a recession for the class?"

"My apologies. It's my 18th birthday today, and I can't stop thinking about it. If I remember correctly, a recession is defined as a period of declining economic performance across an entire economy that lasts for several months. It typically affects Gross Domestic Product (GDP), household income, employment, industrial production, and wholesale-retail sales."

"Good job, Mr. Bell! Brains, basketball talent, and business acumen! Now pay attention or meet me in detention! Birthday or not!"

I spent the remainder of the school hours trying to concentrate in class while wishing time moved faster than usual so I could go home and see Grandma Lindsey's gift.

The bell rang, and I immediately made a dash for the door. To my surprise, I met my Mom at home. She had cancelled her classes and was home earlier than expected.

"Welcome home darling and a happy birthday to you!" she said as she hugged me. "I forgot to do that this morning."

"Thank you Mom; let's get down to business. Where's Grandma's gift?"

"Young King, why the rush? The gift ain't goin nowhere."

Mom brought out the cake she'd made (her cakes were the best), and we sat down to devour it after she had promised to show me what Grandma Lindsey got for me.

Halfway through, I asked, "Hey Mom, signing is in three weeks, and I haven't made a decision yet. Any help?"

"What do you have in mind?" she asked.

"I don't know. I have to choose between going to college and going pro."

"Why pro?" she asked.

"It's pretty obvious, Mom. I'll be able to help you. Going to college will only make us spend more money. Pro scouts are calling me the left-handed Kobe Bryant. They're even saying that I could have a similar type of career if I come straight out of high school. Without a doubt, I can be drafted top 5 and start earning big bucks immediately with my rookie contract and endorsements," I replied.

"I see, but do not worry about me Jah". I promise you that I will be fine and most importantly happy with whatever decision you make," she said. "I have a little something for you. It's on the living room table; can you get it for me?"

"Sure, save some cake for me though," I said as I headed for the living room.

On the table was a card placed in between a Jet Magazine and a Black Enterprise Magazine. Ironically, they were Grandma Lindsey's favorites.

I picked up the card and found a letter addressed to me. I gave Mom the letter, and she opened it, revealing its contents. There was a picture of me and my grandparents at Reginald F. Lewis University in Virginia. It was the university's homecoming. We had taken a picture on the football field with the band members and dance team after the half-time show. My grandparents were big donors to their alma mater, and because they always loved watching HBCU bands perform during half-time, they often got the perks of being on the field with the band. Per usual, there were also more boring stock certificates and savings bonds which Mom put back into the envelope for me.

"I'll put these into your trust and custodial account," she said.

"Is this all what Grandma Lindsey got for me?"

"She's got a lot for you. In due time, you'll see the value of these. Be patient, Son. Patience is all it takes."

I wondered why Grandma Lindsey didn't come as promised. I still hoped for a better gift and suspected Mom was hiding something from me.

"Oh yeah, silly me I almost forgot.", Mom said jokingly, "She also sent you those sneakers you'd been asking for to go with those stocks. They are on your bed."

"Yes, I knew it! Grandma never lets me down!" I said.

* * * * *

The next week, Mom unexpectedly had to go to Greenville, North Carolina for some "job." I figured something was up, because she never took tutoring jobs outside of Newark. The fact that it was in the same city where Grandma lived was fishy as well. When I asked if I could come with her and see Grandma Lindsey while she went on her job, the look on her face was telling. She vehemently refused and ordered I stay put.

I promised I would stay back, but I was not one to back down. Something just didn't feel or seem right. As soon as she was gone, I grabbed my hoodie, a gym bag, my wallet and trailed her. A new-found benefit of turning 18 is that I am now able to purchase long distance business class bus tickets without an adult. I got on the same bus with her and went to the back, making sure she didn't see me. I couldn't help but feel anxious as the bus kept riding along the highway. I wasn't sure if I was anxious because I knew something was up with Mom, or if I didn't want to get caught. It was probably a little of both. I tried my best to stay hidden in the seat. That way, if she moved towards the back of the bus to use the bathroom, she wouldn't notice me.

The drive seemed longer than normal; it was probably just the anxiety. I was wondering so many different things. I couldn't help but think Mom was in some sort of money trouble, or worse, she was seeing some man all the way in North Carolina. All I knew was that while we were here, and after I had come all this way, I was going to see Grandma Lindsey before I went back home. Besides, she had some explaining to do about not showing up for my birthday... even though I had no idea how I was getting back home.

The bus finally came to a stop, and I watched Mom get off and walk towards the hospital. At the hospital door, she stood for a while throwing glances before entering.

I felt extremely silly and thought to myself "Maybe she did ride all the way here for work." Nevertheless, I kept my distance as I followed her inside to find a phone to call my Grandma to come pick me up.

"Hello, my name is Jah-Regal." I greeted the lady at the reception. "I'm looking for a....."

She immediately interrupted me, not allowing me to ask my real question. Instead, she suggested that I must be here to also see Dr. Lindsey Bell. For a moment, I was shocked. I could not breathe. It all started to make sense.

"Go straight down the first door to your right. You'll find her room there. We are all praying for her and your family. She means a lot to this community," she said.

It all became clear to me. This is the reason why Grandma Lindsey couldn't make it for my birthday. I immediately felt guilty. I had wanted her to come so bad I forgot what she was going through. It has been six months since Papa Bell passed. It must have been tough for Grandma Lindsey, and the heartbreak must have started to take a toll on her body. I stood at the entrance and watched Mom tend to her.

"Mom," I called as she turned, shocked that I was there.

"Jah! You shouldn't be here. I made you promise you wouldn't."

"I just couldn't bear it, Mama. How's Grandma Lindsey?"

"She's holding up. She will be back on her feet soon. She just needs rest. She's small, but we all know just how tough she is, Jah."

I went over to Grandma's bed and planted a kiss on her forehead as a tear streamed down my cheek. She smiled, caressed my hand and called my name, "Jah-Regal," my "God of Kings." She never wanted me to see her in this state, but I could tell she felt at peace now that I was by her side. The nurse came in to check her pulse and asked us to leave her to rest a little.

A week later, Grandma Lindsey passed away in her sleep. It was my Mom and I against the world now;

Grandma was gone. I couldn't curb my tears. As they flowed freely, I kept replaying over and over the call I received from my Mom as I was leaving basketball practice. Listening to my Mom on the other end trying to hold back her own tears as she couldn't bear to tell me my beloved Grandma had transitioned on was simply devastating.

After the funeral, Grandma Lindsey's lawyer came around. He informed us that Grandma had written a will. This was not surprising, since she had acquired much wealth in her earlier years. When the time came for the will to be read, all of the intended family members came together for it. The family members were not shocked to hear that Grandma Lindsey had willed most of her properties to my Mom and me. I was her favorite and only grandchild. This was obvious with the way she was so fond of me when she was alive.

Grandma Lindsey left us the family farm in Greenville, NC, Papa Bell's car, and a retirement account. I was personally given a $250,000 life insurance policy, which my Grandma Lindsey had put in a trust and instructed her lawyer to give to me when I turned 18. The lawyer also gave me some savings bonds, a check to pay my tuition, an old step van truck and a letter from Grandma Lindsey which read:

Dear Jah,

Our lives should be lived not avoiding problems but welcoming them as challenges that will strengthen us so we can be victorious in the future. When you know The Most High, there is nothing to fear.

Your mind is the most powerful asset..use it to help you create and multiply, never to fear!

I'll be long gone to the world beyond when you read this letter. I have left you a $250,000 whole life insurance policy, a check to cover tuition at any college or university as long as it's an HBCU, some of my top dividend paying stocks, some savings bonds (yes, more stocks and bonds!) and old equipment we used on the family farm.

They can be redeemed by you only if you follow the terms that will be given to you by my lawyer.

What I could not accomplish in life I have done in death. I trust you'll pay it forward.

I love you!

~ Grandma Lindsey

P.S. - Yes, I know you don't need tuition money. You've excelled both inside and outside of the classroom and will be receiving scholarship offers. However, remember true wealth is not defined by money. I left you these monetary gifts, because I wanted you to have two of life's biggest gifts: options in life and the freedom to make choices without having to worry about money. I know you will make the right decision.

The lawyer explained the contingencies Grandma Lindsey listed before I could receive what she had left for me.

She stated that I must go to an HBCU, like she and Papa Bell did, and enroll in a financial literacy course which would teach me the basics of money management, budgeting, saving, debt, investing, and giving to avoid many of the mistakes that lead to lifelong money struggles. We always talked about how my Dad's life insurance policy wasn't sufficient enough to provide for me and my Mom after he died; this was one mistake Grandma Lindsey never wanted me to make. She also wanted me to acquire assets, start a business, buy real estate, get a retirement account, obtain life insurance, invest in the stock exchange, and have an emergency fund set aside to cover the financial surprises life may throw my way. Lastly, which I felt was awkward, she said I had to get involved in politics.

Going straight to the pros was out of the picture since Grandma Lindsey wanted me to go to college. In school, I heard a friend say he was considering HBCUs such as John Merrick University, Earl Graves College and Mary Ellen Pleasant University. I had told Mom about it and, as a graduate of an HBCU herself, she supported the idea. A simple search on the internet informed me that Earl Graves College in Atlanta, GA was the best of the best. Their basketball program, which had made them four repeat champions in the league, was one of the best in the country. They basically owned their conference. They had a coach that once played in the pros and was known for being great at developing and preparing players. For 20 straight seasons, they had not had a losing record in conference play. They also made multiple National Tournament appearances within the past few seasons. Even before the conference slate started, they played against top Division 1 teams. The program alone had sent their share of student athletes to play professionally across the world. The campus was also located in the middle of a major city which would increase my exposure in the local community.

The day of the signing soon came and to everyone's surprise, I picked an HBCU, Earl Graves College in Atlanta, GA. It was time to make my Grandma proud as well as start my own legacy.

MINDSET BEFORE THE MONEY

The next day before class, I met with my mentor and guidance counselor, Dr. Rani Morris, who has been like a father to me since my father passed away.

He has always been someone that I could lean on when it was time to discuss difficult situations. I usually went to him to help sort out thoughts and make tough decisions. Sometimes just to vent. Sometimes to get perspective and feedback.

Maybe it was from his years of extensive training to become a licensed counselor or maybe it was because he came from a similar background. He was also from a low-income family and lost his father at an early age. From our similarities, we've been able to form somewhat of a father-son bond.

Before school started, I decided to stop by his office to discuss the recent events that had transpired.

Dr. Morris was always a big advocate of HBCUs. He attended a 2-year HBCU where he received his Associate's degree, then transferred to a 4-year HBCU to get his Bachelors of Science in Psychology. Eventually, he was able to obtain his Doctorate degree as well. I never could understand why or how a man with such prestige, and what appeared to be a lot of wealth, ended up as a high school counselor. He'd started a club for Black males at my school and would occasionally take us on HBCU Tours.

"Jah, it's mighty early, what do I deserve this pleasure?" He said, taking a sip of his Tanzanian Coffee from a mug that read, "Cast Down Your Bucket Where You Are - Booker T. Washington."

As he puts down his newspaper, I noticed the title of the article, "Investors & Entrepreneurs Prepare For The Great Recession."

"Hey, Dr. Morris," I responded. "Got a minute?"

"Uh huh," said Dr. Morris. "Anytime you start off with that question, I know it's gonna be more like an hour. Uh oh, you're finally coming in here to tell me you decided to become an Iota man."

Dr. Morris was a proud member of Iota Phi Theta Fraternity, Incorporated, a historically Black, intercollegiate Greek letter fraternity founded on September 19, 1963 in Baltimore, Maryland.

We couldn't help but chuckle. "No really, what's on your mind? Wishing you would've chosen my alma mater, Robert Reed Church University instead of Earl Graves College?" Dr. Morris asked jokingly.

"You wish," I chuckled back. "I mean, it is a beautiful and prestigious campus with an amazing band, but I still have to consider my basketball career Dr. Morris..."

As we began to talk, I couldn't help but see the many framed awards throughout his office. I even saw pictures of him with prominent figures and a very abstract painting with Marcus Garvey, Amos Wilson, Malcolm X, A.G. Gaston, Kwame Nkrumah, Nina Simone, Thelonious Monk and the Obamas.

"Interesting photo," I said observingly. "I've never noticed it."

"Yeah, that's because I just completed it. I've decided to get more into Black art. I painted it myself. All people who have inspired me. But like I said, what's on your mind, Jah-Regal? I know that look."

"So this recession, do you think it's something that we should be worried about? They say it could be worse than the Great Depression."

"Jah, I hate to sound like an opportunist but great fortunes and empires are built during recessions. It's all about perspective and preparation. Besides, when did you become a business guy?" Dr. Morris chuckled.

"I've just been paying more attention to what's going on in the market. My grandparents have left me with a lot to think about. They're stretching me, but in a good way."

We spent a few minutes catching up. But, I really wanted to know the first steps I should make towards becoming an investor and an entrepreneur so I asked my next question. "What do you know about investing and entrepreneurship?"

"Oh man, those are my middle names!" Dr. Morris exclaimed. "The first thing I tell people, though, is make sure you understand the mindset that it takes. It really requires a mental paradigm shift."

"A mental what?" I asked, confused.

"A mental paradigm shift." He says as he hands me the book, "Dream Big. Dream Often. Dream Unrealistic.: Guidelines To Get Off The Sidelines" by two HBCU graduates from North Carolina.

"Make sure you read it! It's necessary to understand what I mean by mental paradigm shift! The first chapter in this book addresses that. For the sake of time, I do not want you to be late for class, so let's discuss mental health first and then the investor and entrepreneur mindset." He said.

I must admit, I was surprised to learn that Dr. Morris addressed mental health and mindset being the first things to consider. I usually thought that once you got the capital and skills required to start, that you could just go ahead and do what you wanted. But Dr. Morris countered this. He began to share a story with me about a client who came to him some time ago. He'd started a business, but along the way, he discovered that he was not taking care of himself or his mental health.

"For starters, investors and entrepreneurs think differently from consumers and employees."

"But we all have to consume. And aren't you an employee?" I asked him.

"Yes and yes. We have to consume to meet our basic needs, but if you manage and invest your money properly, your investments can pay for even your most basic needs. You see, I'm more of an investor than an employee. I work here to help kids like you. This has always been my passion. I once read the book, "Countering The Conspiracy To Destroy Black Boys," I knew I needed to make some career changes. I learned that it is easier to pour into the youth than it is to heal adults. I could be making way more, but I do this out of love. The money that I'm "leaving on the table" by not working a fancy, high paying job, my investments and businesses more than make up for it."

"Jah-Regal, in addition to being a high school counselor, I'm a real estate investor and a venture capitalist. I use the money from each of these opportunities to take care of my basic needs and my life of luxury."

I was surprised Dr. Morris was sharing all of this with me, but I couldn't help it; I was intrigued.

"You should never get a job or a degree because it pays a lot. That is one of the worst things you could do! It might sound cliche, but ALWAYS love what you do. You can find a way to make money if you're a smart investor. A toxic job and work environment can make you sick. There are financial, emotional, physical, and definitely mental implications over time. Let's address mental health first, and then, we'll discuss the different mindsets. Your mental health is important, Jah. I wrote an article about mental health and hating your job."

I was amazed. The conversation had become more than I had bargained for when I came to see Dr. Morris, and I was loving every bit of it. Sitting there, listening to him talk, I was in awe of everything that he had accomplished. I couldn't even put into words how excited I was to be getting all of this knowledge. It reminded me of the conversations I used to have with Grandma Lindsey.

There was so much Dr. Morris was sharing with me about the importance of taking care of your mental health that I had never considered. He shared some of the signs that can show someone isn't happy with their job. I would've never thought that lack of sleep, getting tired easily, headaches, unstable mental health, becoming ill, and even loss of appetite could be related to being unhappy at work. One good point Dr. Morris made was that it is dangerous to try and persevere through adverse work conditions when you know the job doesn't favor you. He really made me understand just how important mental health really is.

I'd gathered a few more valuable points on the mindset of an entrepreneur. Just looking at the notes that I started taking was almost overwhelming.

> *Move for Independence: Oftentimes, we see that most entrepreneurs are very smart. Their qualifications can certainly land them better jobs than they can imagine. However, they choose to experience the rough road of starting their own business rather than working for someone else.*
>
> *Adversity: We see magazines and newspapers graced with the beautiful stories of people who have actually made it to the top*

as entrepreneurs. They often have these perfect pictures that fail to talk about the challenges and roadblocks they've overcome before getting to the top. This can affect an entrepreneur's mental health if he is not aware of the potential difficulties that he will eventually face.

Time Consuming: For your business to grow, it is important to give unlimited attention to the work. You will have to be willing to sacrifice some of your personal time.

Growing Responsibility: Every entrepreneur's ultimate goal is for their business to grow. Growth comes with extra responsibility and new challenges. In the face of these new challenges and opportunities, the entrepreneur is always expected to be strong even when the pressure is on his or her shoulders. This can become a burden if you are not mentally prepared.

Founders Eat Last: The foundation for growth of any business is the ability of the entrepreneur to give all they can for the business to succeed. In order to foster business growth, the entrepreneur will often give incentives to his workers even when it might not be convenient for him. He leaves whatever remains for himself. He just has to put his business and employees first.

Financial Risk: Before any business can operate, there is a need for a financial investment. It is just a necessity. 20% of businesses fail in their first year. When a business fails, it typically leads to some type of financial crisis for the entrepreneur.

Dr. Morris spent time going over all of these points with me. Earlier in the meeting he had mentioned that mindset is equally as important as what he invests in or what business he eventually starts. "Before considering becoming an entrepreneur or an investor you have to train your mind and understand the differences." Dr. Morris explained.

He even took an extra step to state the differences between being an entrepreneur and being an investor. "You have to ask yourself, Jah-Regal, do you want to be an investor, an entrepreneur, or both?" He inquired.

I couldn't help but ponder the question for a moment. "I'm not sure I really understand the differences between them, Dr. Morris."

"Well, let me explain." He offered. "The entrepreneur is a risk taker. The entrepreneur is one who sacrifices everything he has in order to create a business. Entrepreneurs stand the chance of either making a huge fortune or losing everything they have ever worked for. By their very nature, entrepreneurs tend to see things in terms of possibility. They are visionaries; they see things that others can't see. In some ways, entrepreneurship is a spiritual journey. This is the reason behind most inventions we see today."

I was intrigued. "So what about the investor?" I asked.

"An investor, on the other hand, has limited risk. They put in capital that they can afford to lose. They go into investments just for profit. They usually have no personal attachments to the businesses they invest in. And by their very nature, investors tend to see things in terms of opportunity. They get to be the judge of why things will not work out the way they should. This might be seen as being negative, but it is important to say that this role is very necessary. This prevents entrepreneurs from going into opportunities that will swallow their businesses."

"Wow. That's a lot to take in Dr. Morris. Which one do you think is better?"

"Well Jah, it's important to state that none of these approaches can be seen as better than the other. Instead, they serve complementary purposes. Without one, the other will find it difficult if not impossible to exist. It is left for the person involved to choose which one is most preferable to serve his or her life purpose." He continued, "The most important thing is your mindset. You have to have a healthy mindset to start a business. Not everyone knows how to obtain and hold on to that healthy mindset, but here are a few things that have worked for me."

I knew the conversation was going to continue to provide me with the knowledge I needed to do exactly what my Grandma asked of me. I made sure to keep taking notes as Dr. Morris talked. By the time I was done, this is what my paper looked like.

Learn To Take Advice: One key feature to being a good entrepreneur is the ability to seek advice from others and apply it. Many entrepreneurs forget that there are experts who possibly know more than them in their given industry. The problem that comes with this kind of mindset is that common mistakes that are made could have been prevented simply by seeking and taking advice. It is very important to ask for help when necessary and not make decisions blindly. The sustainability of your business depends on this.

Sell Yourself: Everyday we are selling something, even ourselves. Selling yourself is a skill that everyone must learn. No matter what you do, you must be able to communicate your perceived value to others. It is very important that you get comfortable with selling yourself if you want to be a great leader and entrepreneur.

Project Management: Before one starts a business, they should be willing to share and delegate their responsibilities to others. An entrepreneur can never do everything or know everything. There are times when they will need to outsource and delegate tasks to their team. By doing so, they will have more time to effectively and profitably work on multiple projects at once.

***Build a Network:** As an entrepreneur, you should be willing to expand out of your comfort zone and surround yourself with diverse, like-minded people. There is a saying that goes, "Iron sharpens iron" and another that states "We are the average of the five people we spend the most time with." As much as building a network is important, it is also critical to be connected to people who can actually offer and get you what you need. It's not about how many people you know, but rather the quality of people you know.*

***Set One Goal:** Entrepreneurs will often make a long list of the things that they want to achieve, but many of them will not happen. Not because of a lack of motivation, but because there was a lack of planning. One way to prevent this is by setting one goal at a time. This might sound like mediocrity, but it is the right step to take. Instead of making a long list of things you will have to do, it is better for you to take one very intentional step after the other. This way, you are able to preserve your mental stability while actually making moves that matter.*

CHAPTER TWO

I left the meeting with new energy and motivation. I learned much more than I thought I would before going in to Dr. Morris' office. By the time I left, I was ready to go home and create a few plans and ways to ensure that my mindset and mental health would stay healthy when I started to embark on my journey. I couldn't wait to start my journey as an entrepreneur and investor.

HBCU LIFE

My flight from Newark to Atlanta was two hours and twenty minutes long. As we approached for landing, I hoped my luggage would quickly greet me in baggage claim. I'd packed my suitcases the night before with all of my fly gear: 2 suits, 20 shirts, 10 pairs of pants, and 10 pairs of shoes, including the ones my Grandma Lindsey gave me for my 18th birthday. I planned on buying some new clothes to add to what I'd already packed once I got settled in Atlanta. I also carried something else with me: Books, books, and more books! I was tired from the farewell party that my family and friends threw for me, so I'd slept during the entire flight. But I woke up just in time to see my new paradise beneath me as the airplane descended onto the runway.

"Click!"

I took a picture with my phone to capture my first memory of Atlanta.

This was nothing like Newark! Coming from a place where almost everything is at odds with my being, Atlanta seemed to be the breath of fresh air that I needed.

I instantly felt at home as if I were just two feet away from my mother, because I was hit with the sudden realization that I was going to be surrounded by like-minded people from all different walks of life. And the best thing about it was, even though they looked like me, we were diverse in complexion, socio-economic backgrounds, religion, political beliefs, and more.

I didn't explore the city much during previous visits, but I knew just how beautiful Atlanta was through what I saw on the internet and TV. I was excited about the opportunity to finally visit The APEX Museum and learn more about the artwork in The Hammonds House Museum. I couldn't wait to see the different masterpieces hanging on the walls. I really couldn't wait to visit both The King Center and the Martin Luther King, Jr. National Historical Park so I could pay homage to one of my heroes. I also knew that I had to find a way to see the amazing skyline of the city.

I had seen pictures of the campus, but nothing could beat the feelings of fulfillment I experienced arriving here! For too many reasons, Earl Graves College (formerly Earl Graves Negro Institute) holds a special place in the educational evolution of Black Americans. Like Most HBCUs, it was established before 1964. What made EGC so fascinating was that it was one of the first HBCUs founded by Blacks in 1857. It was built by a collective effort of free Blacks and newly freed slaves in Atlanta. The first class had three teachers and sixty students. Over the years, more and more Blacks heard of the college and began to attend. As the college expanded, it was able to acquire over 200 acres of land. Today, it is known as one of the most prestigious private institutions in the country.

In addition to having a winning basketball program, ECG is known for producing top Black business leaders. Specifically, they have produced almost half of the 12.5% of Black CEOs in America and more than half of the 32% of HBCU graduates working in the venture capital (VC) industry. As I walked across "The Yard," I was filled with an immediate sense of pride in attending an HBCU. I thought about the legacy of trailblazing women and men who had stepped on each of the 107 HBCU campuses throughout the history of our great institutions. I was now a part of that legacy. I especially felt a great deal of pride for attending EGC. The school's motto, "Pushing the Family, Community and Culture Forward," resonated with me because my parents and grandparents had always stressed the importance of doing just that. It only took minutes to realize that I'd chosen the right path for many reasons.

HBCUs were founded to provide higher education to Black students who wouldn't be accepted elsewhere, and also less privileged people in society, including whites and other races. Historically Black colleges and universities tell a story of love, acceptance, and more importantly, resilience. They are a signal to the entire world that if being black meant one thing, it meant rising up despite intentional trips and falls — after being beaten down. Most HBCUs started from unconventional places: people's homes, churches, and small buildings. And in less than a century, they were taking their place among the most prestigious universities in the world.

On a personal level, for me, attending Earl Graves College meant I had somewhere to stand. A place I could leverage to amplify the voice I was trying to find within. Being a Black man is a constant struggle. Even now in the 21st century, many of us are just seen and not heard. And I am one of them. I had a story to tell, and I'd been my own audience so far. So when I knew that HCBUs were waiting for me, I concluded that, of course, I would answer the call and share my story. My reality.

I did have concerns and fears. I couldn't help but think that something might stop my expression of the dreams and imagination I held inside. Even more, I feared that the sabotage might come from myself. Unfortunately, fear was something embedded in my mind from life's experiences, disappointments, pain and now my decision to go to a small HBCU over a top Predominantly White Institution (PWI) or the pros. The fear of being forgotten, even before starting, and somehow not living up to Grandma Lindsey's legacy were my biggest fears. The fear that somehow, I might not be good enough to prove myself right and everyone else wrong. My fears tended to come like shockwaves. One moment, I was bold and down for anything. The next moment, I'd be reconsidering the other side of good. The other side that no one talked about.

But as I entered the campus, the feeling was different. I passed by a group of girls who were probably the most beautiful women I had ever seen in my life. Then, a guy passed by me going in the opposite direction on a skateboard. And, I almost bumped into a guy kicking a soccer ball and rapping loudly to one of my favorite rap songs. I saw a young lady handing out two flyers, one for a Greek step show and another for a pre-dawn gym jam. My stomach growled as I walked past the cafeteria. It smelled similar to my Mom's popular fried chicken. At that moment, I couldn't help but think, "God, I'm going to murder today's "Fried Chicken Wednesday".

✶ ✶ ✶ ✶ ✶

As I walked into my dorm room for the first time, I noticed how bright it was. Just the way I loved my room back home. The view of the city from my room in Newark would be one of the things that I was going to miss most about home. My dorm room was empty, and the windows were half open. However, one side of the room already had someone's possessions there.

"Dang it. Dude lucked up and already got the good side of the room." I said.

"Oh well." I thought to myself as I stared defeatedly at the twin-sized bed that would be mine for the next two semesters. I crouched by the bedside for a moment before collapsing onto the unsheeted plastic mattress.

"Man, it's been a long day! And judging by the feel of this twin bed, an even longer year. But, it's whatever! I can't believe that I'm finally here. In college. Dad. "Pops". Grandma. I'm a college student!"

I laid there for some minutes before forcing myself to start unpacking. I opened the suitcase and started arranging my clothes, books, sneakers, hats and video games on the dresser and small shelf. As I was hanging up my Ervin Johnson poster, I heard someone walking in and say, "Wrong MJ! But, Hi anyway!"

"Hey man, what's up?" I responded.

"You must be Jah-Regal. Jah-Regal Baldwin? And apparently, you're a Lakers fan."

I chuckled. "Jah-Regal Bell. Nah, I just love Magic. The greatest to do it on and off the court. And you are . . ."

"James McCarthy. And as you can tell, I'm a fan of the other "MJ" from North Carolina!"

We both chuckled.

"Nice to meet you brother." I said. We shook hands and dapped each other up. "You just got here too?"

"No, I've been here since yesterday. I heard you were from Newark."

"Yep. And yourself?"

"I'm from Greenville."

"Oh cool. North or South Carolina," I asked.

"North," said James.

"Dope, I have family in Greenville, North Carolina as well." I said. "I guess we're already like family. How is North Carolina? Got a girlfriend back home?"

"NC is hot this time of year! And yeah. Her name is Morning. She decided to go to another college. We're going to try the long distance thing," said James.

"You know what they say about long distance college relationships, Bro." I said.

"Man, not you too" James sighed.

"Nah, I wish you both much love and success." I said.

"What about you? You're a star athlete. I know you have a girl or two?" James asked.

"Nah, I've always been too busy with basketball and my books. Been focused on getting my 10,000 hours in," I said to him. "Besides, that's the beauty of college. The possibility of one day finding my Whitley Gilbert here," I chuckled. "Either way, I'm good, but it would be dope."

"Who is Whitley," asked James.

"C'mon, Bro. Dwayne and Whitley are a classic HBCU power couple. I have the complete series in my DVD collection over there. You need to binge watch every season and episode before the first day of classes." I said jokingly to James.

We laughed and talked well into the evening getting to know each other. I even gave him the nickname, "J. Mac".

We talked about our first homecoming. Walking "The Yard" for the first time. Our first party and concert. Possible Greek life. Stepshows. Student protesting and student government. Studying abroad. The best rappers. He thought I was crazy when I said Master P was one of the best rappers alive but I explained to him how Master P turned a $10,000 life insurance policy into a family empire and his views on Black ownership. We later went on to discuss the current rap beef and the past east vs. west coast rap beef with much laughter between them. I was sure that my time at Earl Graves College (EGC) wouldn't be boring after all.

We both talked about how we've always been focused on being good students in the classroom but hoped that attending an HBCU would also allow us to focus on learning more about Black culture, history and most importantly, being Black males.

I learned that James was on the golf team. It was the first time that I'd ever seen a Black golf player in real life.

By the end of the conversation, I could tell that we were both from different rungs of the economic and social ladder but we still had a lot in common. I had a feeling that "J. Mac" was going to be a lifelong friend. I'd been so focused on basketball and helping my family that I didn't have many friends in Newark. Back in high school, all the socialization I'd ever engaged in were either at church or at basketball practice.

"Anyway, I need to get some sleep. We're supposed to meet with our academic advisor err..." I rushed into my pocket for a piece of paper, "Dr. Annette Kornegay tomorrow in Oprah Winfrey Hall. You know the way around?" I said.

"Yea, I'm familiar with Oprah Winfrey Hall. Plus, I hear that Dr. Kornegay is super cool."

* * * * *

A banana, an apple and a donut is all I had time to grab from the cafe for breakfast before going to Dr. Kornegay's office. We arrived at her office a bit early.

While waiting, I took a walk outside to look at the morning sunshine. My Grandma Lindsey used to always say that the sun is our friend and we should spend more time in it. "The Yard's" lawn was perfectly groomed. I noticed that the band was up practicing. The drums from the band were always my favorite instrument to hear. I sat there a little longer watching the band practice before I found my way back towards Dr. Kornegay's office. I walked up to James just in time.

"Mr. Bell, could you please come in?" said Dr. Kornegay.

I recognized the face of my advisor. Much different from what I'd seen in pictures though. She looked much younger and prettier in person, yet very distinguished. I entered the office, unsure of what we would discuss in our first meeting.

"'This is your first time in Atlanta, Mr. Bell?" Dr. Kornegay asked as I sat in the chair before her. James sat in the chair to my left.

"No, ma'am. I came here for my campus visit."

"Mr. McCarthy?"

"Came here in junior high…to the botanical garden on a biology field trip."

"Oh. Great. You must have noticed, then, that this city of ours is quite a busy one. And many students that come here think they have to spend to keep up with the Joneses."

"What does that mean?" I had to ask.

"Joneses could mean many things, Jah-Regal." She adjusted her glasses. "It could mean following fashion trends, hosting parties or…"

"Buying every sneaker in town!" James cut in.

I cut my eyes at James, but didn't respond. I simply nodded and waited for Dr. Kornegay to say more.

"And that is why I make financial management the first introductory session with any student who walks in here. I have discovered, during my twenty-three years of practice as an academic advisor, that the first trace of academic derailment is linked to many things; one of which is poor financial management. I'm sure you both understand me up to this point?"

We nodded.

"Learning to manage your finances early in your college career will help set a strong financial foundation that you can use for the rest of your life. Here is what you need to know. The best way to get more is to manage what you have. Don't spend more than you have to, and never spend all that you make."

"With all due respect, Dr. Kornegay, neither of us are making any money right now." James and I said to her while looking at each other.

"Well my focus today is to introduce you to a program that we started here at EGC called 'HBCUNomics'. The goal is to give you tips on helping you survive financially during your time here instead of just living off of your parents or off of your refund checks. We hope that by planting these financial seeds now, it will help with the rest of your tenure here and well beyond college." Dr. Kornegay continued. "At EGC, we want you to have a producer mindset instead of a consumer mindset. You both will one day become high income earners. But did you know that you could start making income now?" she asked while handing us an 'HBCUNomics' pamphlet. "Today, we'll talk about the eight types of income streams."

"Sounds like it's gonna be a long day." James whispered.

"Most likely." I mumbled.

"At the top of the list here is what we call earned income. I'm sure you know what that means guys. James?"

"Errm, when you get paid for a service. I changed my Dad's flat tire once and got paid 20 bucks."

"Bingo!" She searched through a stack of thin books on her table. "Excuse me, please." She soon found the books and handed each of us one. "Yes. Earned income could range from tips, wages, and salaries to net income from personal establishments. It requires that you work before you get paid for your service. A little sweat equity. Make some physical and mental contributions to the business at hand, and you get paid. Then, you have profit income. On the surface, this looks quite familiar to earned income, but in the real sense of it, they are very different. Profit income is the leftover financial gain after the cost of production has been removed. For example, James, what you got from your Dad does not count as profit income because the extent of your input has not been measured and monetized to show if you have made a profit or a loss. Imagine if the energy dispersed during the process of changing a flat tire can be measured, then we can determine if you were underpaid or if you made a profit. So we can say that profit income equals total income minus total expenses."

"Awesome stuff." I said.

"Definitely. So that brings us to the third income stream which is interest income. Basically, interest income is earned from investment accounts. This includes earnings on fixed bank accounts, savings accounts, and Certificates of Deposit (CD's). Next, is residual income. This sort of income is the net income that an investment can yield at given percentages over time. Basically, these are investments where people have percentages of shares that will continue to yield revenue without additional physical input."

Dr. Kornegay stood up from her chair and paced up and down the room while her assistant brought us bottles of water. She gave us a five minute break to digest everything she'd just shared with us before continuing on to the next topic.

"The next type of income is dividend income. This income refers to the distribution of a company's earnings to shareholders that own a percentage of that company. You can become an owner of a company by purchasing stock," said Dr. Kornegay.

"Oh wow, my Grandma purchased stock for me from several sneaker companies! I guess that makes me an owner too!" I said.

"That's absolutely right!" said Dr. Kornegay. "Besides this, there is passive income. One example of gaining passive income would be through rental properties, both residential and commercial. The income generated from rental properties goes to the landlords who rent out their homes to other people who are known as tenants. Capital gains income is another one. This is defined as the increase in value of an asset.

"Assets?" We both asked.

"My apologies, said Dr. Kornegay. Yes, an asset is something that makes you money. While a liability is something that takes money from you."

"If you want to become wealthy, you should quickly learn the difference between the two." She stated with authority.

"And remember, it's not how much money you make, it's how much money you can keep." She insisted before continuing on with her original points. "These assets are mostly from the sale of a property, land and/or some form of investment. The capital gains income is only received when the asset has been sold. It is important for you to know that assets decrease and increase in value due to the nature of supply and demand and the economic activities around the properties involved. Did you know that most cars decrease in value roughly 30% as soon as you drive off the car lot?" She asked.

James and I had no idea!

"And the last one here is royalty income. Royalties are primarily payments made to rightful owners of things that are used over a specific period of time. In exchange for a royalties payment, you are granted permission to license or to make use of other people's intellectual property... mostly artwork, copyrights, patents, trademarks, designs, books, etc. Do you understand this Jah-Regal?"

"I do, ma'am."

"James?"

"I understand."

"Alright. One must then ask a very important question in this regard: How can students manage their finances and maximize it for generations of income? As students, here are some useful tips for you..."

✲ ✲ ✲ ✲ ✲

When we got back to the room, I flung myself on the bed, practically exhausted from the meeting with Dr. Kornegay and the tour that followed. After we left Dr. Kornegay's office, we hit the streets of Atlanta, taking pictures, and sightseeing. I called my Mom before going to sleep to tell her about my day. I excitedly told her about everything I had learned from Dr. Kornegay and my time touring the city. Mom said she was very proud of me, and I let her go so she could get ready for her next work shift.

I decided to look over the financial management handout Dr. Konegay gave me before I passed out. The list was long, but I managed to read through it. Here's what it said...

HOW TO MANAGE YOUR FINANCES AS A STUDENT

1. ***Budget Your Income:*** *Create a detailed spreadsheet of your fixed monthly income and expenses. Also document the exact amount of every single purchase (outside of your fixed expenses). Understanding the flow of your expenses and your spending patterns will help make your budget as realistic as possible. This will prevent you from making irresponsible financial decisions.*

2. ***Avoid "Keeping Up with the Joneses":*** *Living an expensive life should be your last priority as a student. This is the time to build a foundation where your money works for you, not against you. Remember this advice: live a simple life now, so you can enjoy luxury and comfort later.*

3. ***Invest More, Save less:*** *Investing grows your money faster than saving and is a much more realistic option for every student. If you put your money into a savings account, your interest yielded will be very low compared to a productive investment account. Consider this question. Would you be able to keep $500 in your account without touching it? Or does putting your $500 in a*

safe and secure investment that will yield higher returns sound more strategic?

*4. **Avoid Accumulation of Bad Debts:** Bad debts will quickly ruin your net worth (assets minus liabilities), and they should be avoided at all costs. This type of debt includes excessive use of payday loans, store cards and credit cards with high interest rates. Bad debt also involves taking out loans for depreciating assets like new cars, clothes, trips, and electronics.*

*5. **Open a Bank Account:** Every student should open a checking and savings bank account. You'll need a place to safely deposit your paychecks. It also helps with making direct deposits and paying bills online. You can use your bank account statements to help budget and track your income.*

*6. **Train Your Mind:** To be able to follow the instructions in this document, the most important element is that you train your mind the right way. Believe me, the mind is where battles are won or lost. And if there is only one battle for a student to win, it is the battle of responsible financial management. Practice these teachings daily, and your mind will have the discipline it needs to live a financially prosperous life.*

Reading the last few words of the handout reminded me of my earlier conversation with Dr. Morris about mindset. I focused my thoughts on his words and drifted off to sleep.

CHAPTER FOUR

ENTREPRENEURSHIP

As days went by, it became obvious that the visit with Dr. Kornegay was very impactful. Our conversation inspired me to do further research on ways to generate income. My Grandma's mandate about starting my own business continued to replay in my head. Starting my own business would be the perfect way to start receiving earned and passive income.

I had just made it back to my room from basketball practice and saw James sitting at his laptop lost in thought.

When James was silent, he was either staring into his laptop programming codes, watching lectures or reading a financial accounting book. On the other hand, when James was excited about a topic, he could talk about it for hours, and this was one of those times.

"YES! Finally. Seeing the light in the darkest situation is what separates a successful person from an unsuccessful one." Shouted James. "I leveraged my computer programming experience from high school and developed an algorithm which I use to monitor finances. I just merged technology with finance," he James.

"Bro, what are you talking about?" I asked. "Better yet, the way you're always studying, don't bother explaining. Just make sure I'm a client of your firm one day."

We both laughed.

"Honestly, I suck at budgeting. I don't think there's anything that could stop me from buying all these sneakers and hats. I love sneakers. Haha!" I chuckled.

"You just earned yourself a free consultation on assets and liabilities. You will be my first client," said James.

After our conversation, I started frantically scrambling through all of my stuff like a mad man, searching and searching for a book my Grandma had given me. James wondered what book might be so interesting.

"Hey man, what's up with you?" James said as he chipped in to help me find the missing book.

"Yo, did you by any chance use any of my books?" I asked without looking up.

"Oh, that's right! I grabbed one of your books for my business class. It seemed like it had a lot of useful information. My bad man, I forgot to tell you I had it."

"No worries. I'm just glad I didn't lose it or leave it in Newark. Just tell me next time, so I'm not looking crazy in here." Relieved, we both giggled.

There are few things I care more about than my sneakers and my books. Especially ones given to me by my grandparents and my Dad. They are extremely sentimental and keep me connected to my values.

The entrepreneurship book I was searching for discussed how to start low risk, low cost profitable businesses on any budget. While reading, I stumbled across something about how to start a mobile food business. The more I read, the more it highlighted how the industry is experiencing massive growth and how it is projected to be a multi-billion dollar industry by 2023. Mobile food entrepreneurs were already experiencing waves in major cities in states like Texas, California and even in Washington, DC. This was intriguing, particularly since this was the perfect business concept for a college campus. Students literally eat at all times of the day and night!

I remembered the old step van truck Grandma Lindsey left me. I could leverage that equipment and my Dad's mechanic network and convert the step van truck into a mobile food truck. Not only was it a low startup cost option, but I also read that with the right concept, preparation, processes & systems, it could be recession proof.

I spent the rest of the evening locked up in my dorm room eating Maple BBQ wings, studying, and dissecting the mobile food business industry, consumer spending habits, and possible recession proof concepts.

The next morning, I bumped into James in our kitchen.

"Hey James! There is something I want to talk to you about."

"Same here." James said. "Jah-Regal, I met a beautiful Queen in the cafe last night at the pre-dawn party. I think I might've found the one bro!"

I chuckled, "Ever since your break up with Morning, it seems like every week you've met your potential wife."

James was a sheltered preacher's kid. Aside from coming to school to get a degree, his other two objectives were to find a wife so that he could also have a long successful marriage like his parents and to have kids. Clearly, I had more things on my mind than to hear his story, and I'm sure he could tell that I was anxious to run my thoughts by him.

Sensing this, James just gave up and asked me to go on.

"You know after our visit to Dr.Kornegay's office?" I started. "I've been wondering what I can do to create additional income for myself and jobs for other students. It would also help my Mom at home."

"Interesting. So, what did you come up with?"

"I was reading that book, and I came across the idea of starting a mobile food business.

"A mobile food business?" asked James.

"Yeah, you know a food truck. Something to do on the weekends, late night, and holidays." I explained.

James was impressed, at least he was not stuck with a dummy after all. Though he would have preferred a more lively and outgoing roommate who enjoyed attending parties, he was impressed that I had big dreams and aspirations.

"I think it would be great if you spoke to Dr. Kornegay about that. Maybe she will have some advice for you." James advised.

"Yeah, I'll do that. I'm thinking of naming the business 'Your Wingman,' and I'll sell my family famous chicken wings and donuts. The name is inspired by my Dad who passed away. When he was alive, he called me his 'Wing Man.' Every time we hung out or needed to have serious talks, we would always make chicken wings, get donuts, and listen to music. It was a weird pairing, but it was our thing. We would talk about many things which most kids would not ordinarily discuss with their parents. My favorite quote by him was simple yet profound, "Do the stuff that works and stop doing the stuff that does not." He shared a lot with me, especially about the difficulties he was having keeping a job without a degree. We were literally best friends up until his death. Despite him not leaving a lot because of the difficulties he faced in keeping a job, he left many memories, and I want to honor that as much as I can...our relationship and his love for music."

For a moment, James stopped to think. I could tell he was wondering why I suddenly wanted to start my own business. I knew it could seem sudden to someone else, but it really wasn't that sudden at all, not to me at least.

"You know, my grandparents onced owned a lot of successful businesses back in North Carolina, including a restaurant." I said, almost as if I was reading his thoughts.

My grandparents were great entrepreneurs in their community. All through my childhood and adolescent years, they stressed the importance of starting a business of my own. They owned a successful restaurant which had been, and still is, a great source of income for the family. They always said: "If you are going to get into business, start a recession-proof company in industries such as food, beverage, retail, technology, health services, or service and repair." When I was in high school, I spent some of my holidays helping out my grandparents in their restaurant. They taught me that no matter how bad the economy gets, people still have to eat. So I acquired the background knowledge and experience needed for a related business. Establishing a restaurant can be very expensive though, which is why I decided on a less capital intensive food truck venture. Having a food truck would provide me the opportunity to run my own restaurant with almost half of the overhead costs, and more flexibility, mobility, and a competitive advantage to maximize profits.

"You know you will have a place bigger than this when you grow up." I could hear Grandma Lindsey so clear. She used to say this to me whenever I helped out in the restaurant."

For a business to thrive without much hiccups, there had to be good planning and execution. I decided to sign up for entrepreneurship mentoring and workshops at The Center for Entrepreneurship and Innovation (CEI) at EGC. It is a hub for entrepreneurship education on the campus. The center has a record of producing the best entrepreneurs in the community. This would also help me satisfy my grandparents' entrepreneurship dreams for me. A food truck might not be the whole vision, but it was a good start.

Strolling through the alley that led to the CEI, I saw many monuments in honor of great entrepreneurs. They had quotes engraved on them. One in particular stood out and caught my attention. It was a quote by A.G. Gaston. It read:

"Money is no good unless it contributes something to the community, unless it builds a bridge to a better life. Any man can make money, but it takes a special kind of man to use it responsibly. "

At the entrance of the center, there were pamphlets which were put in a rack by the side of the door. I helped myself to one. On the inside flap of the pamphlet was the mission and vision statement of the CEI:

"The Earl Graves College's Center for Entrepreneurship and Innovation is very diligent in its mission. Today, we see that most universities have adopted entrepreneurship studies because it is critical for one to be self-reliant. Aside from the personal development that comes from working for yourself, it contributes a great deal to society. The CEI has a major goal which is to ignite students' entrepreneurial passion and equip them with the knowledge, skills, connections, and practical experiences needed to be successful innovators and entrepreneurs in whatever path they may choose."

In the CEI center, students have access to hundreds of entrepreneurs and professionals that can help them better navigate various career paths. They also work closely with a group of retired executives of successful businesses. This group is known as the Service Corps of Retired Executives (SCORE). They partner with the Small Business Administration (SBA) to make sure that the students have all they need to open a successful business.

Learning about the SBA from the pamphlet, I made plans to contact them in order to get help with my food truck business. Coincidentally, there was an ongoing business counseling program, and some of the members of the SBA happened to also volunteer as mentors. I jumped at the opportunity to join. It was great. They provided me with helpful tips and encouraged me to relentlessly pursue my business goals.

The SBA mentors also gave me a list of things to consider when starting a business, more specifically, a food truck business. One of the volunteers owns a brick and mortar restaurant now, but he started off with a food truck, just like I wanted to do. Here's what we discussed:

WHY PEOPLE DECIDE TO START A BUSINESS:

People today have many reasons to start a business. However, it is important to have the right drive when beginning the entrepreneurial journey. This is because oftentimes, the drive shapes the line of action you will follow when trying to achieve certain goals. When you have the wrong drive, it will affect your decision-making process, which might end up ruining the business before it has a chance to become successful. A few things the members of the SBA identified as the driving force behind many businesses are: the need for independence; the need to follow one's passion; job creation; alternatives in fundraising; the pride that it gives' the respect that comes from it; or just the desire to make money.

"Coffee or tea?" One of the attending SBA counselors offered just as I was about to pour some for myself.

"Yes, tea please. I'm not a big coffee drinker." I replied.

He chuckled. "If you stick with entrepreneurship, coffee will become your new best friend, Mr. Bell."

After a short break, we moved on to the next topic.

HOW TO START A FOOD TRUCK BUSINESS:

Like any successful business, starting a food truck requires some planning to help the owner achieve his or her desired outcomes. First, you should draw out your concept plans using a business canvas model. Then, you need to get incorporated and licensed, if applicable. This allows the business to operate in your city, county or state. After that, you need to get a truck and make sure that you can finance the upfront expenses through your own capital or using other people's money (OPM). Lastly, you will need to obtain permits for parking spots and to expand the business as time goes on.

One mistake that food truck owners make is that they include too many options on their menu. The SBA counselor helped me create a simple menu for a chicken wings and donut food truck business. It was an odd concept, but I just knew it would be a hit!

YOUR WINGMAN MENU

TRADITIONAL AND BONELESS WINGS

* Hawaiian
* Garlic Parmesan
* Lemon Pepper
* Hickory Smoked BBQ
* Maple BBQ - The best seller
* Spicy Honey
* Mild

Louisiana Rub
Mumbo Sauce
Spicy Korean
Original Hot
Old Bay
Old Bay Honey

DONUTS

Glazed
Chocolate Frosting
Strawberry Frosting
Buttercream Frosting
Sprinkled Donuts

Once we finished creating the menu, we shook hands and parted ways. More than ever, I was feeling excited about how everything was starting to come together. The thought of creating a unique experience for people that included good food and music reminded me of my family. Being able to package that feeling and present it to my community and campus meant a lot to me.

Out in the lobby, I sat down to review some of the things mentioned in the meeting. I needed to write them down before I forgot. The brother I sat next to stretched his hand out towards me just as I started writing.

"Malcolm," the stranger beside me said while shaking my hand.

"Jah-Regal." I replied, plainly trying to get back to my work. But Malcolm still had more coming for me.

"I see you have an interest in being an entrepreneur. Hope the session went well?"

"Yes, thanks." I replied, trying so hard to get back to my notes.

"If I may ask, what business do you have in mind?" Malcolm began.

At this point I had to just accept defeat and plug into the conversation.

"Food truck."

We spoke for a while, and I found out so much about him. Malcolm was a graduate student from Baltimore finishing up his MBA/PhD. He was part of a joint-degree program offering an MBA in combination with a PhD in sciences. Malcolm was in the process of getting his MBA from another HBCU, Herman J. Russell, which is the top MBA program in the state and his Ph.D from Asa Philip Randolph University in Data Science. He had already graduated with a Bachelor's degree in Computer Science from Earl Graves College a few years back.

When I mentioned my own area of interest in the business world, Malcolm also let me in on his plans.

"You must really love school." I couldn't help but say.

"I love knowledge. I plan to run the first Black billion dollar tech company one day. I need knowledge to reach that goal. Applied knowledge is power. I first started my tech company back in undergrad out of my dorm room. As soon as I finish with my dual program, I will be running my company full-time," said Malcolm.

My mind exploded with questions as soon as I heard Malcolm say 'billion dollar tech company.' I couldn't help but think that I was meeting this brother for a reason, because I definitely had plans of becoming a billionaire myself.

"Technology is here to stay and data is the new real estate," he continued. He offered to help me understand some of the ways I could apply technology in my own venture. I couldn't help but be drawn to the discussion after that.

"Most definitely." I responded to the offer.

"I will help you set up a website and an app. But in the meantime, I will teach you how you can use pay-per-clicks and sales funnels, and I will also teach you how to automate your social media and processes."

'What do you mean by pay-per-click, sales funnels, and automation?" I asked with confusion written all over my face.

Malcolm responded with a smile and explained the concepts. He said that pay-per-click is an internet advertising model which is used to attract traffic to a website. He further explained that an advertiser places an advertisement on your site and has to pay the owner of the website for each click that he gets on his ad.

"Then when we talk about social media automation...." Malcolm continued, "there are tools that help people build their social media presence through content curation and will schedule their social media posts in advance. This frees up more time for the owner to have more authentic interactions with their customer base."

Malcolm shared additional benefits of using technology within my business. Among the benefits he identified were things like being cost effective, reaching a wider audience, building a customer base and drawing the attention of potential investors.

"And hey, at the very minimum, make sure you have these three things: a website, a company email address, and a social media page if you want to be taken seriously. Social media pages are the wave of the future." Malcolm added.

Beginning to feel a bit hungry, I thanked Malcolm for his help. Before I left, we exchanged contact information so we could stay in touch.

"Thanks again for everything, Malcolm. I owe you! Hey, you never know, one day I might even become one of the first investors in your tech company!" I shouted as we parted ways.

CHAPTER FIVE

REAL ESTATE

It was a beautiful Saturday evening. I had been out busy with the new food truck. All of the tips and advice people had given me were really paying off. I'd been able to achieve some financial stability since I started.

"Hey James, the day was good..." I paused as I opened the door that led into our room.

There was this pretty young lady seated with James. When I first saw her, all I could think of was how beautiful she was. She was 5'5 with a pecan tan complexion and long braids. I noticed the elephant pin on her blazer. She had me frozen, but I regained my composure and walked slowly into the room.

"Hey!" James returned. "Meet my friend, Rachel-Rani."

"Just Rachel will do, James!" Rachel said.

I wasted no time inserting myself into their conversation; "Why not Rani? Rani actually means *Queen*." I extended my hand towards her for a handshake. "Queen Rachel, I'm Jah-Regal!"

Trying to hold back her smile; "I know who you are, the freshman basketball phenomenon turned 'food truck genius'," said Rachel.

Rachel was a 20 year old real estate agent and investor. After completing her associates degree from O. W. Gurley Community College (a 2 year HBCU), where she studied Finance, she then transferred to the local women's 4 year HBCU, Ida Wells College, to study pre-law. Her goal was to become a real estate lawyer. Right after high school, Rachel got her real estate license so she could create a job rather than working for someone while she was taking classes at the community college. Her parents always stressed the importance of sound money management, having a plan for your life and investing.

James had contacted Rachel knowing the passion I had for my business. It was his own little way of helping me expand. Rachel had been a friend of James, so it was not difficult convincing her to come speak with me.

'Well, I have a movie date. I'll leave you two alone for now," James said picking up his jacket on the arm chair.

"Another date, huh?" Rachel asked.

I couldn't help but chuckle at her sarcasm and James' relentless pursuit for love.

Rachel and I proceeded to talk further to get more acquainted. I couldn't help but notice her shirt, "Ambitious. Audacious. Creative. HBCUEducated. Fearless. Original. Unapologetic. Entrepreneur. Investor."

"Dope shirt!" I said. I looked down at her elephant pin. A coincidence and maybe even a sign, but both her and my Mom were Deltas.

"You know my mother is a Delta too." I said smiling.

"Wow...that's nice," she responded. "A smart lady," she winked.

Delta Sigma Theta Sorority, Incorporated is a Greek-lettered organization of college-educated women devoted to helping those in need with a focus on programs that accommodate the Black community at large. Delta Sigma Theta was founded on January 13, 1913, by twenty-two female students in Washington, D.C.

Currently, Rachel was working part-time as a commercial real estate agent.

"James told me all about your food truck business. You know I admire people who know what they want and go after it." Rachel said.

Though Rachel was casual in her demeanor, I couldn't help but feel a tingle run up my spine. I really admired her and wanted to get to know her better. That aside, I maintained my composure.

"Thanks. Just trying to make ends meet while living up to some expectations." I finally said.

'What do you say I fix you up with a store front? A little expansion won't hurt." Rachel offered.

I wasn't sure how to respond. However, business was booming, and it was time to consider expanding. I thought to myself, "Expansion will only create more overheard." My Dad used to always talk to me about

Parkinson's Law, or as the late great poet The Notorious B.I.G. once said, "More money, more problems."

Rachel actually understood. She didn't seem the least bit surprised by my fears at all. But, she pressed on with her offer to help. I don't know if it was at that exact moment or not, but I knew she had a thing for me too. I noticed that she tried to cover it up the same way I did.

After showing me many properties, she eventually sold me on a three-unit storefront and explained why it is smarter to get a storefront with three units rather than just one. A three-unit would increase my potential for more passive income and future capital gains because of the developing area. I was a little apprehensive at first, because it was an expensive move with a lot of financial risk. She told me her motto was "Dream Big or Stay In Bed," meaning always stretch yourself. Hearing this motto helped me make up my mind. I knew the three-unit storefront would pay off over the years to come. Before letting Rachel in on my decision, I thought I'd run it by James first, since he was the numbers guy.

"Well, how about I think about it and get back to you." I quickly said. I was eager to hear what my roommate thought.

To reassure me, Rachel shared some of her background which included learning from her Dad who was a local real estate mogul and who had taught her everything she knew.

"Whenever my Dad was closing a deal, he brought me along. So I've been an intern for over a decade."

Rachel had a real estate portfolio that consisted of properties she acquired using a Real Estate Investment Trust (REIT) as well as homes she had purchased with tax deeds and tax lien certificates. The properties included single family homes, multi-family homes, and commercial real estate.

"So you used a REIT to invest in properties?" I perked up.

"Oh yes!" Rachel explained, "A REIT is a company that owns and operates commercial real estate that generates income. This allows an average investor to diversify his or her portfolio and own multiple properties."

"Wow," I said. "So what kind of properties are in a REIT?"

Rachel continued, "That's an awesome question! Properties included in a REIT portfolio may range from apartment complexes, data centers, health care facilities, hotels, cell towers, energy pipelines, office buildings, shopping centers, self-storage, and warehouses. One benefit of REITs for investors is that it gives them a chance to own a portion of real estate that will consistently yield income."

"So how did you purchase these properties?" I asked. "Did you use a conventional loan?"

Rachel replied, "I've gone the conventional route for a few of my properties. However, where I've seen the greatest return on my investment has been in properties that I've purchased below market value. I bought those using either tax deeds, tax lien certificates or creative financing."

I sat in silence for a second trying to process what I had just heard. Then, I asked, "Would you mind breaking that down? It's really a lot to take in."

Because of her passion for real estate, Rachel lit up. She could talk about real estate all day! "Of course, I don't mind!" said Rachel. "A tax lien certificate is a certificate which is issued to real estate investors. This certificate gives them claim over a property on which a county or municipality has placed a tax lien as a result of the owner failing to pay taxes on the property. The tax lien certificate is sold at an auction to the winning bidder. The winning bidder pays the delinquent taxes to the county or municipality, and then has the right to collect the unpaid tax amount plus interest and penalties from the property owner. If the homeowner redeems, or pays off the tax lien during the redemption period, the tax lien is removed, and they maintain ownership of the property. If the homeowner does not pay the unpaid taxes and interest, the tax lien certificate holder becomes the property owner."

"So you can really purchase a property for the amount someone owes in property taxes?" I asked.

"You sure can." said Rachel. "Tax deeds work in a similar manner." She continued. "The main difference between the two is that, when it comes to a tax deed sale, the county or municipality actually transfers ownership of the property by deed to the winning bidder at the public auction. So, there is a higher chance of becoming an instant property owner at a tax deed sale. Depending on the state where the property is located, there may or may not be a timeframe where the homeowner can pay off the taxes and get the property back. In any case, once that redemption period passes, or if there is no redemption period, the winning bidder becomes the new owner of the property, and the prior owner's interest is wiped away." One thing to consider is that tax deeds range in price from a few thousand dollars to tens of thousands of dollars. So, it is a more capital intensive investment."

"Sounds like an investor can come up on quite a deal in both situations." I said.

Rachel replied, "That's certainly been the case in my experience! What's even more exciting is, although you're getting sweet deals, you're not limited in the types of property you can buy." She explained, "Investors in the real estate business have the choice of either investing in single-family, multi-family, or commercial properties. Diversity in the types of investment property you have in your portfolio is important, and it is often said the more doors you own, the more passive income you will receive."

I responded, "Well that makes sense."

She was so excited that I understood what she was talking about, she continued. "A single-family home is a property that has a single tenant or one family residing there. On the other hand, a multi-family property typically houses more than one tenant and consists of anywhere between two to four units. Single-family properties usually involve individual houses, while multi-family properties are often seen in the form of duplexes, triplexes and quadplexes, which are two, three and four unit townhomes. What becomes an issue for most investors is which property type to pursue."

A feeling of enlightenment came over me. I wasn't sure why, but Rachel had fully captured my attention. Although food trucks were my *thing*, I wanted to know more. "So what about apartment complexes? I didn't hear you mention them."

"Well apartment buildings are residential properties because most or all of their income comes from dwelling units. However, mortgage lenders consider any residential building that has more than four units to be commercial investment property since they are generally bought and sold strictly because of their ability to produce income. Non-residential commercial property is any structure or land that is used to generate income, typically with the use of lease agreements. Included in this category are office buildings, medical centres, hotels, malls, retail stores, farm land, warehouses, and garages." She finished with, "One day, I will put together one of the largest commercial deals ever."

While Rachel scrolled through her phone, showing me brick and mortar properties, I was attracted to the best storefronts I saw.. But Rachel had a better plan.

"Here! This is what I think you should use," Rachel said, handing over the phone to me.

The storefront was an UGLY but spacious, brick, 2-story, located perfectly in the center of downtown, where new development was happening in the city.

"Ahhhh.....why not the fancy stores?" I questioned.

Rachel proceeded to teach me the benefits of buying the ugliest property in the best location. Over the years, such areas are redeveloped and experience gentrification. Besides the increased property taxes that result from redevelopment, the restoration of these areas becomes an added bonus to those who have owned property there all along. Property owners also get to see an increase in their property values. As an investor, if you are able to get in at a lower price point before redevelopment begins, when or if you decide to sell, you will be able to demand more for your property. In turn, you will receive a larger return on your investment.

She went on to explain that I should create a separate Limited Liability Company (LLC) for each unit in my potential storefront. "Doing so will limit your personal liability and protect your personal assets from any debts of the business. You will also be personally protected in the event a lawsuit arises." Rachel said. "It is very common for investors to use an LLC to invest in real estate. Not only will an LLC protect you from potential liabilities that arise during the course of business, but it will also provide a framework for determining ownership of any property held by the business."

Rachel showed me the specs for the property, adding that each store within the building has the potential to rent for $700 per month.

"Ok so, here's the thing...having a store is a nice idea, Rachel, but the problem is getting the funding I would need to buy it and fix it up," I admitted.

"The property is listed for $50,000." Rachel stated. "But, I'm sure he'll sell it for less."

"What....who?" I asked.

"My father." Rachel said. "He's always giving back to other young guys trying to make a difference. Plus, I'm his daughter, this is my first sale this month, and I own part of this property." She chuckled. "He can never tell me no. Besides, I love your ambition, and you're kinda cute. Plus, I'm rooting for you, Black man!"

Rachel explained that due to the current recession, both commercial and residential real estate were on the market for super cheap. She said subprime and adjustable-rate mortgage (ARM) loans had affected the real estate market badly, causing it to take a turn for the worse.

Subprime loans are loans which are given to individuals who fail to satisfy certain credit requirements. These loans have higher interest rates and come with a lot of risk because of the potential for the borrower to default on the loan payments. On the other hand, an ARM is a type of mortgage in which the interest rate on the outstanding balance varies at different points during the life of the loan. With an ARM, the initial interest rate is fixed for a period of time and changes at certain intervals. Massive defaults on subprime loans and ARMs led to the great recession we were currently experiencing.

"Rachel, how about dinner tomorrow night?" I asked confidently.

"It would be my pleasure to have dinner with a 'food truck genius' and now a fellow real estate investor," said Rachel.

We exchanged numbers. I could hardly contain myself when she left. As soon as the door closed behind her, I realized how hard my chest had been beating the entire time. She was bound to be my wife! I could already tell. I couldn't wait to tell James when he got back to our dorm room. Now, it was my turn to be excited about meeting a girl.

COMMUNITY BANKS

After deciding to buy the storefront property from Rachel and her father, I now needed to finance it. Since the property is less than $60,000, I had to obtain a personal loan instead of a mortgage loan. I would use the loan to purchase and renovate the storefront. Rachel also explained to me that it would help build my credit if I got a small personal loan instead of using cash.

Rachel introduced me to Kwaku John, a Finance Manager from Ghana who worked at William Browne National Bank, a Black-owned community bank across from the school. It was named after the founder of the first Black owned bank in America.

"Hello Kwaku," Rachel said as she extended her hand to greet the dark, slim brother sitting on the bench.

"Hi," replied Kwaku, almost jumping from where he sat with excitement.

Rachel apologized for keeping him waiting. She didn't waste any time introducing us.

"Jah-Regal, this is Kwaku. Kwaku, meet Jah-Regal. He is the one I talked to you about over the phone." She said.

"Oh....a pleasure meeting you." Kwaku said with his thick accent.

"Same here." I replied with my eyes browsing the suit Kwaku had on. In the privacy of my thoughts, I couldn't help but think, "That's a nice suit!"

"Rachel has already given me a brief introduction on the importance and advantages of working with a community bank such as yours rather than working with the big banks." I added. "She also highly recommended working with you because your bank is intentional about lending money to qualified local black businesses and entrepreneurs."

Community banks are depository institutions like any other bank. But its ownership and operations are carried out locally. Someone might wonder why Rachel suggested that I work with a community bank rather than going with the many other options that were available. The advantage that community banks have over other commercial banks is that it is operated by locals who understand the plight of the people. This enables them to shape their policies in such a way that accommodates the life of the everyday small business owner. Because I am a student with no substantial income outside of my scholarship, I am able to claim 75% of the revenue generated from my mobile food business.

As Kwaku was printing the necessary documents to get the loan application started, I asked about his background. I wanted to know more about him, like where was he originally from, how he ended up in America, and where he got his creative name?

Kwaku went on to tell me about himself. He was from Akosombo, a small town in the Eastern Region of Ghana. He moved to America to attend college. After graduating from college, he decided to stay and pursue a career in banking. He was inspired to work at a smaller banking institution, such as community banks, because growing up, his family always participated in a "Sou Sou." He saw first-hand how a small amount of cash could make a huge impact in a family and a community.

"What is Sou-Sou?" I asked.

"Sou-Sou refers to a group of people who pool their money together by making regular deposits to one fund, which is then paid out to participating members of the group according to an agreed upon schedule," said Kwaku.

He then explained to me how he got his name. In Ghana, children are named according to the day of the week they were born. For example, males and females who are born on Sunday are named Kwasi or Kwesi (male) and Akosua (female). Kwaku was born on Wednesday and his name matched that day of the week.

Rachel decided to break the long conversation that was building between two new-found friends.

"Errmm......guys, I have a place I will need to be in the next hour or so. Can we jump into business and leave the whole catching up thing for later?" Rachel sarcastically said as she pulled gently on Kwaku's jacket.

"Yeah, that's right. I almost forgot." Kwaku replied with his usual calm voice.

"Well, I've explained to Jah-Regal why choosing a community bank over a big bank works in his favor." Rachel chipped in trying to steer the conversation.

"Ohh...that's good. Now, I will say a few more things concerning that." Kwaku began.

As he began to compare the differences between the two kinds of banks, I took out my notebook so I could take notes on everything he shared. It was a lot! Here's what Kwaku explained:

> *1. Community Investment: In local community banks, the money deposited by customers is used as loans for small businesses and investors in the surrounding areas. This gives these investors and businesses a chance to grow which leads to an increased employment rate of locals in the communities. And now, you have a more stable economy. But, when you invest in big banks, your money will be used as a loan for larger companies in big cities that will just expand for their own personal profit. This could potentially block the help that could have come through the community banks for small businesses which would directly impact the local community which you are part of. So choosing a community bank over a big*

bank is a way of giving back to yourself and your neighbors.

2. Support the Local Economy: Community banks are more inclined than larger banks to give back to the communities in which they serve. They can do this by sponsoring local non-profits that are devoted to giving back to the community as well as supporting local fundraisers, campaigns, and schools. This helps their communities become more stable and recognized. Community banks can also commit to community development projects to help provide certain amenities that are lacking. For example, Kwaku's bank sponsored the development of three swimming pools in lower income neighborhoods. They also fund swimming lessons for many families. This is just one of the ways that community banks can enhance local amenities.

3. Better Services: One of the main problems we face with big banks is the bottleneck on which most of their services are based. There are less personal relationships than you would see in local community banks. The community banks help to break the gap that exists between customers and the bank they work with. They are devoted to seeing that your needs are well attended to no matter how big or small. With big banks, you need to be a prominent customer before they pay attention to your needs as they should. This is mainly because these banks are focused on their profit goal.

4. Financial Security: As mentioned earlier, big banks build their goals around profit. This makes them go to any length to satisfy this objective. This also puts the whole financial system at risk when they invest in businesses, that might be seen as "risky," with the money deposited by the customers. Community banks only use these funds as loans which come with proper securities. So the safety of funds are generally better guaranteed when it comes to community banks than with big banks.

5. Keeping up with Trends: In every sector of human life, we strive to find ways by which processes can be made more accessible for users. This is the main reason behind the advancements in technology we see today. Similarly, community banks try to keep up with these trends in order to make their users more comfortable and also give them a sense of belonging in society.

While sitting down with Kwaku, he shared some alternative ways to build credit while still in college. He seized the opportunity to explain some tips, since Rachel was on a long call.

"There are plenty of ways to build your credit."

He continued. "This is important, because your credit score is what banks use to determine if they will work with you in the first place. So, you have to give them something they would like to see."

Seeing the puzzled look on my face, he elaborated.

"First, make sure you maintain a good credit score. Good in the sense that you can show a history of making your credit card and utility payments on time. You also have to make sure that your cash flow is something that is acceptable. Try to keep your expenses as low as possible, and do not max out your credit cards. While you want to show that you know how to use a credit card responsibly, you don't want to look like you NEED one to survive. You want to show banks that you make enough income and revenue to cover your lifestyle, which indicates that you will not be a liability to the bank. It's all about building financial trust."

"So where do I begin?" I asked.

"Getting credit for the first time can be very difficult. As a student, you might just have an opportunity to build your credit by getting a gas card. You can use the card to fill your tank up and then immediately make the payment to your card, so you can start to show a history of making your payments on time. It takes a while to build a good credit reputation. So, it is advised that you take your time and be patient with the process. In most cases, the age of your credit matters. Banks will examine how long you have had your credit lines and how well you have been able to manage your credit."

"Are you guys done?" Rachel chipped in. She'd just ended her call.

"Yes," we said at the same time.

Just as we were about to leave, Kwaku told me that it was important that I learn how to calculate my credit utilization ratio. The credit utilization shows the amount of your credit that is being used. It is important to keep a low credit utilization ratio. This will keep your credit score from decreasing. Your credit score is extremely important if you plan to use other people's money (OPM) such as money lenders or bank loans. Before we left for good, Kwaku handed me a pamphlet about credit utilization. I quickly glanced over the first page:

Calculating Credit Utilization: In order to calculate your credit utilization ratio, you will have to document all of your credit card balances. This will help point out how you have been spending over any given period of time. A recent copy of your credit report can also be useful because it will include all of your account information in one place. Plus, credit utilization factors into your credit score and is based on the information in your credit report, which could be different than your current credit balance. Compare your credit card balances to your credit card limits (how much you're allowed to spend on the card) to make sure that you aren't over-spending. When you have your credit limit, you divide your credit card balance by it and then, multiply by 100. That will give you your credit utilization ratio.

With this, we exchanged pleasantries and went our separate ways.

"I'll see you next time," I said to Kwaku who was waiting for a cab. We shook hands, and I walked away excited from all of the knowledge I'd received.

CHAPTER SEVEN

POLITICS

After the meeting with Kwaku, I walked back to the dorm while Rachel decided to take a cab to her friend's place. I had to pass the giant sculpture that stood in the middle of The Yard of Diane Nash, a co-founder of the *Student Nonviolent Coordinating Committee*. It was commissioned by one of the student leaders in October of last year. This was a beautiful sculpture that students rarely stopped to appreciate. As I was walking by, I noticed a group of students together with various signs chanting and shouting, "I Can't Afford School. Education Is A Right!" "Black and Brown Must Unite." "Vote Our Agenda." "Hold Decision Makers Accountable." "End Housing and Wage-Gap Disparities." I watched them for a second and then walked back to my dorm room.

"Wow...hello guys." I stood at the door looking at a group that had gathered in the room I shared with James.

"Hey." They said nonchalantly, paying little attention to me. No one seemed to be interested in giving me an explanation of what was going on.

They were arranging some papers which I soon realized were campaign posters. James is very active with school politics and was seeking to get elected. He'd tried to pull me along in the race many times, but I wasn't interested.

"Politics? Bro..you know that's not my thing." This is what I would always say whenever James tried to discuss those topics. He even tried to get me to help with his campaign, but I avoided it by staying busy with my business. He wouldn't take no for an answer though. He decided to bring the party to me this time. This is why he decided to hold his campaign meeting in our room.

"Hey man.....come have a seat." James called to me as I was still trying to understand what I was in for at that moment. James pulled up an old box crate from the corner of the room for me to sit on.

"Huh?" That was all I could say because he'd caught me off guard. I reluctantly adjusted the seat and made myself comfortable. James continued on with the meeting. He began to explain why he had called all of us together. He scanned the room as he spoke, but for the majority of his speech, his eyes were fixed on me. He knew how I felt about politics, and I'm sure he could sense my urge to leave the room.

Just as I was about to say "eff it" and leave, I suddenly remembered the many talks that my Grandma Lindsey had with me about the political history of our nation. Grandma Lindsey was no politician, but she made sure she followed everything that was happening in that arena. She occasionally talked about her role and responsibility of being a Black business owner in the community. She believed that Black owned businesses should always bail out Black protestors as needed, provide funding for resources to support Black causes and movements, and contribute to the candidates that supported our community and views.

I remembered that a request from my Grandma was to get involved in some level of politics. This had been her wish for me since I was a little boy.

Grandma Lindsey was adamant that voting on the issues and not the party was critical to the community and building wealth. She told me that almost everything that happens in the community is decided by the political institutions and their "friends." She would go on for hours discussing how policies shaped everything. She would often talk about redlining and how it disproportionately affected the accumulation and transfer of wealth only becoming illegal after the Fair Housing Act of 1968.

"My generation understood the importance of civil rights but more importantly our political rights, Jah. We always voted for a purpose. We voted for the issues and not the party. We made our votes count. We demanded change and action with our voices through peaceful protests, boycotts, votes, and dollars."

It was always her wish that I become part of the political force that makes things happen. And to begin, she suggested that I start to build my career in school politics. This would allow me to create the necessary foundations for whenever I decided to enter politics after graduating. She gave me several other reasons why I should join school politics. As James talked to the group that had gathered in our dorm room, I couldn't help but to reminisce on some of my Grandma Lindsey's reasons:

Dealing with Stage Fright: One of the inspirations for joining the Student Council is to be the mouthpiece for the larger student body. To do this, you will have to speak to different people in different environments. While it may seem scary at first, it helps students develop the charisma that is necessary when they eventually decide to dive into the world of politics.

Opportunity for Leadership Training: When you sit on the Council, you learn what it means to be a leader. You are faced with different personalities and demands, all while making decisions that try to serve them all. It can be tough trying to please everyone; in fact, you can't. As a Student Council member, you learn to accept this fact, while taking pride in knowing that your decisions are helping most if not all students.

Doing Things the Way They Should Be Done: Frequently, students on the Council get to see things and learn about issues that others may not be privy to. This gives them the chance to implement some ideas that can bring about great and positive change.

Circumstances don't have to remain as they are, if they aren't working for the greater student body. By joining the Student Council, you are able to effectively create an environment that serves the students' overall well being.

Reaching Out to the World: As a member of the Council, you get to attend events and meetings. This is a great opportunity for you to increase your network with people who will help you grow. Aside from helping you in your career, you might end up meeting people who will help contribute to your personal life as well.

Inspiration to Do Better: When you become a member of the student council, you actually become someone that is admired by other students. You become a kind of mentor. This will motivate you to do better both in your academics and lifestyle, because others are being inspired by your actions.

Access to Opportunities: One of the main benefits associated with being a member of the Council is the opportunity to meet new and successful people. You also have access to first class information concerning any new opportunity. This, in turn, allows you to establish a solid foundation for your future more quickly and efficiently.

As if the universe was paying attention to the conversations and meetings happening around me, I had my political science class the next morning. The professor, Dr. Hunt, discussed the differences between local, state, and federal governments. My ears perked up. Grandma Lindsey had already put me on game, but a refresh of memory was not a bad idea. Dr. Hunt explained that the different levels of government all work as a process line in a factory. They are components of a whole, yet they have different functions. The federal government serves as a center for all and is the parent government of the other two. It performs the duties in the exclusive list while delegating other responsibilities to the local and state governments.

The state government, on the other hand, serves as the middleman. It brings the federal government somewhat closer to the people. The state government handles the residual duties of the federal government. It is better able to listen to and provide for the people under them.

The local government serves as the closest government to the people. It was established to make sure that the people can be heard from directly. Local governments work to communicate the specific needs of the people to the state and federal governments.

Dr. Hunt shared that the purpose of these different levels is to make sure that the government is brought closer to the masses as much as possible. It also helps in the sharing of duties and resources.

As the class drew to a close, she informed us about a panel luncheon that would be organized by the Business & Entrepreneurship Club and the Political Science Club in the next few weeks. The topic for the panel was "The Roles Of SGA and Student Entrepreneurs." I knew I couldn't afford to miss this opportunity if I wanted to build my political career, my network and my business.

When the day came, James and I attended the luncheon and sat on the front row. The panel discussion was very educational. Both clubs and the SGA walked away with practical projects that each group could work on to help improve campus life for students and to fundraise for Earl Graves College. They had even taken the time to break down the roles attached to different positions in the SGA. I was refreshed on some old information and even learned a few new things about the different roles.

President: The President manages the whole Council. He/she presides over all of the meetings and organizes all of the activities. The President also serves as the representative of the entire student body in different gatherings and in meetings with the administration of the school.

Vice President: The Vice President is the right hand of the President. He/she assists in carrying out the President's duties and is also meant to stand in for the President if for any reason they are not available when needed.

Secretary: The Secretary keeps a record of all the proceedings and activities that concern the Council. This way, important information can be retrieved whenever necessary without much stress.

Treasurer: The Treasurer manages the finances for the Council. This person keeps a record of all of the funds belonging to the Council and how they are being used.

Dr. Hunt happened to be one of the panelists at the luncheon. I learned that she is more than a professor. She's also a local city councilwoman and lawyer. Dr. Hunt studied political science and got her Juris Doctor (JD) from the same HBCU that I attend. She was also the SGA Vice President while she was in school. I was blown away and immediately decided to meet at her office in City Hall the next day to learn more. During our meeting, she explained the role of a city council member, how they interact with the mayor, and how city council meetings work.

Dr. Hunt explained that the city council's interactions and relationships with the mayor depend on the stipulations of the political system. The law points out the power and limitations of the mayor and the members of the council and how they should interact. When the city council has an area of interest, they bring it to the mayor for consideration.

She also explained that she became involved with the SGA and the city council, because she wanted to make a change on campus and in her community using her voice.

While there, I voiced my concerns about how the city needs to become more food truck friendly by rezoning areas downtown and making it easier to get permits. I explained that more food trucks in the city can boost the local economy. I elaborated on how it can create more small business owners, increase employment opportunities, drive tax benefits for the city, and make the city more attractive. Dr. Hunt invited me to the next meeting and told me that I should sign up to speak. She also encouraged me to bring my friends.

* * * * *

I attended the city council meeting with Rachel and some of my friends from EGC and other local schools (HBCUs and PWIs) to collectively voice our concerns. Those who joined me represented student organizations for African-American, Hispanic, Asian, Pacific Islander and American Indian students. We stressed the importance of food truck permits, commercial real estate zoning, diversifying monuments & landmarks around the city, affordable housing for students, safety, and cleanliness around colleges and universities. Afterwards, I felt invigorated, and I was excited about the potential change I could make.

After much convincing and with James' help, I later decided to run for office. To my surprise, I became the first freshman to be the SGA Secretary after a long campaign. I was also the first to unanimously win the position.

That opened the window of opportunity for me to attend my first National Association of Student Affairs Professionals (NASAP) conference over the summer. I was so excited about it.

GIVING BACK

My team and I wrapped up another successful lunch shift which was by far a record sales day with the food truck. As I walked back to my dorm to get prepared for the rest of my day, I was met by the smooth sounds of a young man playing a song from his saxophone from across the yard. It was a song that my father used to play, a Thelonious Monk and Coltrane cover of "Ruby, My Dear." I recognized him as a fellow classmate and a band member. People gathered around him, dropping dollars and coins at his feet.

"I definitely need to add that to the Wingman's music playlist tomorrow." I thought to myself. It brought back so many childhood memories.

I was so moved by the young saxophonist's talent and the memories invoked from the song, that I put the $123.40 that I made from tonight's tips into his dusty fedora hat that sat at his feet. As I continued to walk towards him I couldn't help but notice that he had a sign that read, "Help! Need money for tuition, books, and food!"

Reading his sign created tremendous feelings of humility and gratitude within me. Had it not been for my scholarship, my mother's unwavering guidance, and my Grandma LIndsey'svision of legacy, that kid could have been me asking for help.

I decided to write him a check from my company for $2,500 to put on his student account. I gave him my business card and told him that we should stay in touch and collaborate on a campus Sunday brunch event which would involve featuring his live music with my food truck.

As I got closer to my dorm, I reflected on how I felt that my company and I could be doing more to give back to the local community besides just creating jobs for people on campus.

I could not wait to tell Rachel about today's event and my thoughts. I called her and told her to meet me at our favorite local record store later that afternoon. We'd often meet there to listen to random old school vinyl records together. If we found good ones, we'd add them to my food truck's playlist. I really enjoyed Rachel's company. We could talk for hours about anything. In some ways, she was becoming my new "Wingman" and vice versa. No matter what it was about, we could lean on each other for help and advice.

As the evening moved along, she told me about an after-school program at a local Title I middle school. I was an only child and always wanted younger siblings, so the idea of working with younger kids was going to be cool and rewarding. Since I was becoming a well-known business leader in the community, in addition to being a member of the basketball team, which meant we were expected to have community service hours, I decided to visit the after-school program at the Title I school that Rachel recommended. I didn't know exactly what I wanted to talk about, but I knew that my time would definitely be spent talking to the youth about the importance of entrepreneurship, economics, innovation, and most importantly, chasing their dreams.

A few days later, as I arrived at the school, a young boy and girl, who were obviously twins around the age of 13 or 14 years old, immediately met me at the door. They told me that I was their inspiration. They said they were my biggest fans and had been following me since I was in high school.

Like me, they both had aspirations of growing up to be D-1 star athletes. Unlike me though, they were dominant in more than one sport. They both ran track, and the brother played baseball, and his sister played tennis. They'd started receiving letters from D-1 colleges and universities, but because of me, they now only considered the idea of going to top HBCUs to compete.

"WOW!" I thought to myself. I had been so distracted with my journey that I never stopped to think about the impact that my decision to go to EGC had made on other up and coming players. It was the first time that someone had mentioned to me the power of my decision.

What was even more impressive was the fact that the young boy had been closely following my off court success. Surprisingly, he knew about my successful food truck operation and also wanted to start a food truck business called "Krazy Kookies."

"One day, I want to help create jobs for my family and friends just like you, Mr. Bell," said the little boy. "Krazy Kookies will be the largest cookie food truck franchise." He added.

"Wow!" I said. "Maybe you really are my biggest fan. I'm even more inspired and impressed by you! You have a very mature mindset for someone your age. I'm proud of you young man. But, do me a favor...drop that "Mr. Bell" stuff." We both laughed.

"Be sure to keep your concept simple. Document your processes early, so your operations run smoothly, and remember, the goal is to scale quickly so that you can replace yourself in the business." I offered.

He agreed to take heed to my advice.

The young boy's words about a franchise rang loud in my ears. This was the first time that I'd considered the idea of turning "The Wingman" into a franchise model. Here I was, thinking I was going to be the teacher today by helping the youth, but I was actually learning from them as well. My conversation with the young boy left me with a concept that would actually help me grow and scale my own company without seeking outside investors.

Touched by the conversation with the young man and the fact that the school lacked resources due to being a Title I school, before leaving I decided to write a $10,000 check from my company to the center to help kids purchase computers. I owed it to them!

Title I schools are one of the largest federally funded programs. They were put in place to provide financial assistance and resources to schools with a large number of students coming from low-income families. This is to help make sure that they get what they deserve like many other students. The schools who benefit from this program are selected by the number of students who registered for free or reduced lunch.

While I was having lunch after class the following day, I got a call from an old friend of mine. His name was William and we had attended the same high school back in Newark but had not been in contact since graduation. We definitely had a lot of catching up to do. I discovered that he was at Stokely Carmichael University (SCU), in Washington, D.C., studying Agriculture with a minor in Agricultural Economics. Stokely Carmichael University (SCU) is the most well-known HBCU and one of the top Agricultural Science schools in the country.

What caught my attention most during our conversation were the endowment challenges he mentioned they were having at SCU. As a result, they were going to begin reducing tuition prices, eliminating some academic and athletic programs and selling some of the school's resources and assets the following school year. He talked about how over the years, the SCU found it very difficult to raise funds, get government funding and stimulate alumni giving, especially lately with the recession.

Before our conversation, I had no idea about the disparity in endowments between HBCUs and PWIs.

"This is how crazy it is, Jah-Regal. America has almost one hundred institutions of higher education with endowments of more than one billion dollars and NONE of them are an HBCU. None! The wealthiest HBCU, ranks over one hundred and fiftieth." William said.

"First and foremost, you're super passionate about this, William." I said with a chuckle. "On a serious note though, if you think about it, the main reason it's so hard for our institutions to compete and attract top students is simply because people are not doing more financially to support them."

"We have to hold ourselves more accountable and maximize our individual efforts if we're serious about sustaining and continuing to build the legacy of HBCUs." William said.

Eager to get his opinion, I asked, "So whose responsibility is it to make sure we are getting the financial support we need?"

Shouting into the phone he said, "EVERYONE! If you have benefitted or profited from HBCUs and their culture, then you should financially support them, and not just during our homecomings. This includes the host cities, local government, the university, the parents, alumni and even current students." He continued. "This is why I'm so glad that you decided to go to an HBCU,

Jah-Regal. You're going to do so much, not just for EGC but for the entire HBCU world!"

"I hope you're right, Bro." I said.

"You'll do amazing things for the culture! Trust me!" Said William.

William and I caught up on many other things that we had missed by not staying in touch since graduating from high school. William told me that he finally got a chance to date his high school crush. Her name is Eve. William had been a shy one back then, even scared to say "Hi" to a girl. But as fate would have it, William and Eve both ended up at SCU, and he took full advantage of the opportunity to get to know her better. After a long conversation, we hung up, but not before promising each other that we would keep in touch. I was tired, so I headed back to the room to start preparing for tomorrow's early morning workout.

The conversation that I had with William continued to play in my mind. I wondered if there was anything I could do to help the endowment situation. I started to think of ways that I could start giving back now. Then it hit me, "I'm going to put together a few live music events with my food truck and the band member that I met a few days ago. We can donate some of our proceeds to EGC's endowment and other students needing additional assistance."

The next morning after working out, I went back to my dorm room and told James about the events from the previous day.

He agreed that it was a great idea to put on a fundraiser event, but recommended that I meet with a Certified Public Accountant (CPA) after school that day to understand how this could affect my business. After the meeting with the accountant, I got professional advice on how I could make an impact by giving back to my community while simultaneously helping my business grow. I ultimately decided to start a foundation. The foundation's mission would be 1) to help fund HBCU endowments and 2) to inspire more young Black kids to attend HBCUs to study business or STEAM (science, technology, engineering, arts and math). With these disciplines, they could either start businesses or work in well-paying jobs in the future in fields such as coding, robotics, data science and become donors to their HBCUs.

Before I made the choice to start a foundation, I wondered if it should be a non-profit organization instead. I visited the school's library to conduct some research in order to make an informed decision. While in the school library, I came across an article that helped me clear up the difference between a non-profit and a foundation. According to what I read, nonprofits are organizations that engage in charity programs with the funds that they most commonly receive from the government, institutions, corporate entities and individual donors.

Foundations also engage in charitable missions but not directly like non-profits. They use money from their corporate entities or founders. When these funds are received, they are dispersed to various non-profits for them to carry out the charity purposes for which these funds are earmarked. Some foundations might have non-profits under them through which they carry out their missions. When it comes to funding, nonprofits can receive the majority of their funding from the government, foundations, various institutions and individual donors. Public foundations, on the other hand, are heavily funded by private foundations, corporations and the government. Private foundations rely on individual donors, corporations or family members for funding.

After making my decision, I searched for ways to raise money for the foundation. I spoke to some family members and friends who were willing to give what they could afford to give. I was thankful, but I knew it wouldn't be enough for a large HBCU endowment. So, I contacted large companies to see if they would invest in the foundation. I persuaded them to donate by bringing up the fact that their contributions would be tax deductible. Tax deductible donations are a way for companies to fund charitable and/or educational organizations while taking advantage of tax write-offs. This gives large companies a huge opportunity to support local charities. Some have even been able to deduct 60% from their total taxes.

Starting my foundation brought me back to the requests of my grandparents. I now understood the lesson my grandparents really wanted me to learn. It was bigger than just creating an avenue to generate financial wealth. Instead, it was about pouring back into others and encouraging them to use their gifts, talents, resources, and knowledge to help uplift families and communities. This was my dream for my businesses and foundation, to give back to HBCUs.

I knew I needed to contact Rachel before going further with my plans. She was always coming through with the recommendations I needed to make things happen. I was thankful that she was in my life. Looking at my watch, I saw it was already late at night. I had to catch some sleep and get ready for the next day. Performing well academically, athletically, and in business was stressful! But, I always tended to make the best out of it.

PROPER PROTECTION

When you consider being a student and having a business to run alongside it, I really had a lot to juggle and decide on. At this point, my business needed full attention, and I had to stay committed to finding new and effective ways of conducting my affairs. This, in turn, would maximize business profits. On the other hand, I was getting ready for my exams. Despite having a lot on my plate, I'd managed to maintain a 3.4 GPA. Although my business was steadily growing, I knew that my degree would help open up more opportunities for me to expand.

The saying goes, "All work and no play makes Jack a dull boy." As I juggled the pressure of maintaining a business while excelling academically and being a student athlete, I remembered the days I spent with my Dad while growing up. When basketball season came around, the two of us would always go watch the games. Even though my love for basketball started at an early age, I didn't begin playing basketball competitively until I was in middle school.

I was gearing up for my first national basketball tournament as a freshman. During the regular season, I had led the team to its first ever undefeated season and included our usual regular season and conference tournament championships. It was the first time in school history that we were five peat champions. As a result, I was being scouted as a top pro prospect. During conference play, I led the team in scoring, rebounds, assists and steals, and I am the 2nd overall leading scorer in college basketball. Several pro scouts were projecting that I could be a top 5 lottery pick in the pro draft, if I could lead our team deep into the playoffs.

With this in mind, I knew we must perform to the best of our abilities in the upcoming national tournament. Despite being underdogs, we had a very good team. We've even spent extra time training for it. One day, during one of the practice sessions, while attempting to cross-over the defender, I lost my balance and injured the thumb of my shooting hand. Unable to finish practice due to the pain that was pulsating through my hand, I left the training facility completely petrified. I knew I needed to rest in order for my hand to heal. But, this injury scared me; it was the first injury I'd had since I started playing basketball. It made me reflect on how quickly everything can be taken away. I couldn't help but start to think about protecting my legacy both on and off the court. At least that way, I would have something to keep me going if things with basketball didn't pan out.

Later that evening, after I had wrapped my hand with an ice pack to treat the injury, I laid on the bed pondering, "What will happen if I fail to meet everyone's expectations?" I remembered that it had been quite some time since I had last spoken with my mother. She would always tell me, as a child, that I would be fine when I faced difficulties. I had been busy trying to balance working life with my academics. I finally decided to call my mom for reassurance that everything would be fine. During the call, we reminisced on my childhood and on my Dad, who had introduced me to the game of basketball at an early age.

Every season, my Dad would purchase season tickets to see New Jersey play. At the games, we would often cheer and high-five each other whenever Jason Kidd drained a 3-pointer. Mom also mentioned the journey I've had since deciding to attend an HBCU instead of a PWI. Before I went off to college, my decision was a point of contention between me and the rest of the world, particularly those who strongly believed that if I attended a PWI, all of the resources I needed to prepare me for the pros would be at my disposal.

However, I stressed the importance of attending an HBCU, as it would provide me with an opportunity to be surrounded by people who look like me and who come from similar walks of life, as well as adequately prepare me for the next stage in my journey of adulthood. Eventually, my fans and peers came to terms with my decision. Mom started to tell me that she's been taking free business classes in the Business Center at the local technical community college. I went on to tell her that I injured my hand in basketball practice. She then gave me tips on how to make sure I protect myself next time. I really missed talking to my Mom. For me, it felt like the good old days. "I love you, Mom. Thanks for the chat." I said.

She replied, "I love you too, Son." I promised to never let that much time pass before we spoke again, then I told her goodnight.

After the call, I remembered an interesting phrase that Mom used during our conversation: "From shirtsleeves to shirtsleeves." According to the "shirtsleeves" curse, a family's wealth depreciates as it passes from generation to generation, more specifically, by the third generation. In order to prevent the "shirtsleeves" curse, the first generation of a family that experiences wealth should do everything in their power to create and take advantage of opportunities to set up high cash value life insurance policies, wills, and trust funds that will sustain future generations.

With the "shirtsleeves" curse in mind, it dawned on me that longevity should drive the foundation of every generational wealth-building cycle. This is why I made a commitment to preserve my wealth for my family and future generations. I reached out to a few successful business owners, attorneys and life insurance brokers in the area for mentorship and advice on the best way to go about creating and maintaining generational wealth. They provided me with a lot of valuable information. They discussed everything from asset protection to investment strategies.

INTELLECTUAL PROPERTY

The first business owner I reached out to was Mr. Lee, a mogul in the hospitality and tourism industry. He owned everything from restaurants to breweries to hotels. He told me that if I was serious about being a business owner, then I should make it a priority to do what the wealthy do - protect my intellectual property. Due to the previous conversation I had with Rachel, I was familiar with the term "property" as it relates to real estate. However, I didn't quite understand the concept of "intellectual property."

"Does intellectual property have something to do with your mind?" I asked Mr. Lee.

"It sure does, Jah-Regal." He responded. "Just as the phrase may suggest, intellectual property is essentially the rights that you have in the property of your mind. Of course, it is an intangible property in the sense that it cannot be touched or felt; that is what makes it different from real property or personal property." Mr. Lee said.

I was immediately intrigued. Mr. Lee went on to explain that there are four types of intellectual property: patents, trademarks, copyrights and trade secrets.

"Patents protect inventions and improvements of inventions." Mr. Lee said. He continued, "The United States government grants patent rights to inventors of new, non-obvious and useful inventions. It's basically a *quid pro quo* between the government and inventors wherein the government says 'if you give us this, we will give you that.' As it relates to patents, if inventors disclose their new, useful and non-obvious inventions to the public, this helps promote innovation in our country. As a result, this will lead to the creation of better products and the implementation of better production methods, which will benefit society as a whole. In turn, as a patent owner, you maintain the right to exclusively exercise a limited monopoly over your invention. In other words, for a period of typically 20 years, you get to exclude others from making, using, selling, offering to sale, or importing your invention into the United States. Patents are registered with the United States Patent and Trademark Office (USPTO)."

"Wow, Mr. Lee. This is powerful stuff." I said.

"I know, Son. I actually received a patent on an invention I created to make bread crumbs. I received another patent on an automated bread dough machine. I've been able to make money off of these inventions by licensing my rights in the inventions to other companies. They basically pay me a fee to use my invention." Mr. Lee then pointed to his head and said, "Jah-Regal, everything you need on your journey to create generational wealth is up here. You've just got to use what you have to make the wealth you seek materialize."

At that moment, I was a sponge - soaking up as much information as I could. "Mr. Lee, you mentioned there are other types of intellectual property. Can you tell me about those as well?" I asked.

"Okay Jah-Regal. Let me just say this before I continue. I am in no way an intellectual property attorney. In fact, as a successful business owner, you need to make sure you have a few knowledgeable attorneys on your team. My attorney's name is A.D. Williams, and she's the best attorney I know! In fact, everything I'm telling you about intellectual property, I learned from her." Mr. Lee explained.

"She taught you all of this information?" I asked.

"She sure did." He replied. "And she can teach you too!"

I thought to myself, "I sure can't wait to meet her!"

"Next, we have trademarks." Mr. Lee continued. Trademarks are the type of intellectual property that creates brand awareness. For example, when you see a check mark on a pair of shoes or on a duffle bag, what company do you think of?" Mr. Lee asked.

"Nike." I replied.

"You're right," said Mr. Lee. "Let's try one more. What do you think of when you hear 'Have it your way.'"

After pondering for a second, I responded, "Burger King?"

With a slight grin, Mr. Lee said "You hit the nail on the head again, Jah-Regal." He continued, "Trademarks identify a single source of goods or services. They protect words, phrases, logos, sound, and color. When you see a trademark on any product that a company sells or used in connection with any service that a company provides, the trademark lets you know where (i.e., from which company) those goods or services come from. Trademarks also distinguish the goods or services you provide from those of others."

"In fact," said Mr. Lee, "when you register for a federal trademark, it communicates to a consumer that every good or service bearing your trademark is of a certain quality and is sold or offered by your company. Lastly, having a federal trademark gives you the right, as the owner of the mark, to prevent others from using the same mark or even a similar mark that will likely cause confusion during the course of business."

As Mr. Lee was speaking, I listened attentively. "This is a lot." I thought to myself. "But obviously, I need to know this since he said these tools are used by the wealthy." Trying to take it all in, I asked Mr. Lee "Would I need to own the trademarks, or should my business own the trademarks?"

Looking impressed, Mr. Lee stated, "Great question, Son. Now I see that light bulb going off up there!"

He then continued, "Similar to patents, trademarks are registered with the USPTO. You should register your mark in the name of the entity that will be using the mark. So if your business will be using the mark, then you'll list your business as the owner of the mark. It's important that the owner of the mark is the one using the mark because you don't want to risk having your trademark registration cancelled due to non-use by the proper owner of the mark. Not only that Jah-Regal, but trademarks create business goodwill. Having your business entity as the owner of your intellectual property is attractive to investors. It's also required if you want to franchise your business. In that situation, you are licensing the use of your trademarks to the people who buy a franchise from you."

I replied, "Wow. Is that right?"

Mr. Lee said, "It sure is. Think about McDonald's. Every franchise uses the same golden arches, the same slogans, and also the same menu design. They're only able to do that because they have protected their intellectual property."

I will certainly be franchising my restaurant business, so I need to move some things around on my to-do list. "This is quite interesting, Mr Lee." I responded, while making a mental note to schedule a consultation with the attorney he mentioned.

Noticing the determined look on my face, Mr. Lee chuckled. "Let me tell you about copyrights, Jah-Regal."

Overwhelmed with so much valuable information, I simply nodded my head.

"Copyrights protect the expression of your ideas. You may obtain a copyright on things such as art, written work, music, books, articles, sound recordings, architectural works, and film to name a few. With copyrights, the work must be independently created by the author of the work and must possess some level of creativity. Unlike patents and trademarks, copyrights are registered with the U.S. Copyright Office."

After listening to Mr. Lee, I wasn't quite sure how this type of intellectual property would apply to my line of business. "So in the restaurant industry, how would I use copyrights?" I asked.

Mr. Lee quipped, "Listen, I'm gonna have to charge you a consultation fee for all of this gold I'm giving you, Jah-Regal." We both laughed. "In your business, you can get a copyright on any manuals you create for your employees or for your business in general. You can also register a copyright for your menu designs, any marketing materials, and the information on your website."

It was finally coming together. "Now, I get it." I stated.

"The last thing you should know about copyright protection, Jah-Regal, is that it lasts an extremely long time. For individual authors, copyright protection lasts 70 years after the death of the author. For copyrights that are owned by businesses, copyright protection can last as long as 120 years after the work is created."

I was in awe. "You mean to tell me something can be protected for *that* long?"

Reassuringly, Mr. Lee said, "Absolutely!"

"What was the last type of intellectual property you mentioned? Ahh...secret trades?" I asked quizzically, wanting to make sure Mr. Lee didn't forget to give me the game.

"No, Jah-Regal. It's called trade secrets," he laughed heartily.

"Yes, that was it!" I chuckled.

"Trade secrets protect any information that you use in business which gives the owner of the trade secret an economic advantage over competitors who do not know or use the information."

I asked, "So would this include my recipes?"

Mr. Lee replied, "It sure does! Trade secret information can include recipes, customer lists, formulas, processes, vendor lists, and any other information that is confidential and exclusive to your company, giving you a competitive advantage over others."

"So how do I register a trade secret?"

Mr. Lee replied, "You don't. Trade secrets are essentially a 'do it yourself' form of protection. Your job is simply to do everything in your power to keep it secret. That is what protects it. Trade secret protection lasts as long as the information is kept confidential. However, once that information is made public, trade secret protection ends."

I remembered hearing about the lengths Coca-Cola took to protect its secret formula. Whether it was true or not, legend has it that very few people know the recipe in its entirety. The few people who are privy to this information are prohibited from flying together in case the plane crashes. And the recipe itself is kept in a heavily guarded vault in Atlanta, Georgia! Talk about protecting the secret!

"Jah-Regal, a smart business owner makes sure their business is protected on all fronts. This includes implementing the proper legal documents while they are conducting business. Examples of important legal documents that should be used by business owners include non-disclosure and confidentiality agreements, work for hire agreements, service agreements, and licensing agreements. In addition to these agreements, you want to ensure your formation documents include provisions on who maintains control of the intellectual property of the business as well as how the assets should be distributed upon dissolution of the business entity."

"Well they sure don't teach us this in school!" I exclaimed.

Shaking his head Mr. Lee said, "Jah-Regal, they'll never teach you the things they don't want you to know. You've got to seek out this information on your own. Once you learn this information, you have to apply it. Now that I've passed this knowledge down to you, it's your job to educate everyone you know about the tools used by the wealthy. Ok, well maybe not *everyone*. Just those who are willing to receive it."

At the end of our conversation, Mr. Lee handed me a pamphlet containing lots of valuable information on asset protection. Here's what it said.

> *Retitling of Assets:* Some wealthy families lose several assets as a result of their legal debts. For example, when people own assets in their personal name, those personal assets could be attached to pay off any judgment that is granted as a result of a lawsuit. In order to prevent this, one approach is to retitle your assets. Retitling here means transferring property to an owner other than yourself. For example, if you own property in your personal name, retitling that property so that it is held in the

names of both you and your spouse oftentimes shields that property from the creditor of one spouse, in the case of real property. So if a creditor comes after one spouse for an outstanding debt, that creditor would not be able to place a lien on property that is held jointly by both spouses, unless both spouses are on the hook to the creditor for a joint debt. When property is owned jointly by spouses, it is considered to be held as tenants-by-the-entirety. Here, when one spouse dies, the full title of the property immediately passes to the surviving spouse.

It is also possible to retitle assets from your personal name to your business name. Obviously, this should not be done for the purposes of committing fraud. However, there are situations where individuals own business assets in their personal name. Transferring the title, or retitling, those assets to your business will, in most cases, shield you from personal liability in the event a lawsuit arises against your business (who is now the owner of the assets you transferred).

Getting Insured: *Obtaining life insurance (whole, term, high cash value, etc.) is another method you can use to effectively protect your property. Life insurance allows you to provide for the loved ones you leave behind. It also reduces the tax liability of* *insured properties. In addition, liability insurance can be used to insulate your business from lawsuits.*

Creating Limited Liability Companies: *Oftentimes, companies are over leveraged with debt. This debt can result from outstanding business obligations, such as loans, or civil liability as it relates to lawsuits. In the worst cases, these establishments are forced to shut down. Forming an LLC limits the personal liability of the individual owners of the business. For example, if a business is sued, the owners of the business are generally not personally liable for the debts and obligations of the business. Therefore, any judgment that is awarded for the lawsuit will attach to the assets of the business as opposed to the personal assets of the individual business owners. This added layer of protection is a benefit of choosing an LLC as your business structure. Creating an LLC also has tax benefits that W-2 employees do not have. It's always recommended that you seek professional advice when forming an LLC so you can make sure you choose the most beneficial tax structure as well as satisfy your state's requirements for registering and conducting business within the state.*

Having Irrevocable Trusts: Trusts are another form of asset protection. When a person creates an irrevocable trust, he/she transfers all of their ownership of the assets into the trust. As a result, they no longer have any ownership rights in the assets nor in the trust. Because the trust now owns the assets, those assets will be shielded from the creditors of the trust's creator. This means that in a lawsuit against the grantor (the creator of the trust), the trust's assets will be off limits.

Although the grantor no longer owns the assets now held by the trust, the grantor is able to control what happens to the assets in the trust. A trustee is appointed and is responsible for managing the trust at the direction of the grantor. The trustee also distributes assets of the trust to the beneficiaries of the trust.

Implementing some of these strategies not only protects you from unnecessary losses, but it also creates generational wealth. Having figured out ways by which I could preserve my wealth for generations to come, I realized I would have nothing to actually pass on if I failed to secure my business now. I must also be prepared to take advantage of any wealth building opportunities. To educate myself, I frequently visited both the school and local libraries and searched for strategies to sustain, grow and protect my business and investments. The turbulent economic conditions that this country is currently enduring increased my awareness of the importance of creating a business that will stand the tests of time - even in a down economy. My search was fruitful, as I discovered many effective ways to reach my aspirations while perusing several business-related books and articles. I found more information than I could have ever imagined.

Municipal Bonds: Municipal bonds are loans that individuals or investors make to local governments. States, municipalities, and counties issue municipal bonds to finance its capital expenditures including the construction of highways, bridges, schools, parks or any other infrastructure which the state needs. Municipal bonds are generally tax-exempt when it comes to local, state and federal taxes. Because of this, investors often view municipal bonds as profitable investments. Municipal bonds, also known as "muni bonds," provide a higher return on your investment than what you would receive if you were to simply deposit your money in a bank account.

Real Estate Investments: Real estate investment involves the purchase of revenue generating commercial and residential properties, including land. Investors in the real estate business often buy properties that are in need of repair, fix them up and flip them by putting them back on the market, or they purchase properties for the purposes of holding them and renting them to tenants who, in turn, provide rental income to the property owner. The passive income that is generated from real estate is one method of both acquiring and preserving wealth.

Options: An option is a contract that gives the buyer the right to buy or sell stock at a certain price, called the strike price, by a certain date, which is referred to as the expiration date. An option contract represents 100 shares of a stock. This means the buyer, who pays a premium for the option contract, has the right to buy or sell 100 shares of a stock at a certain price.

There are two types of options contracts: a put option and a call option. Put options allow the buyer to sell the stock at a certain price before the expiration date. Call options allow the buyer to buy the stock at a certain price before the expiration date. In the stock market, the put option can be used as security. It serves as security on stocks which might fall below its anticipated value. This way, the investor gets to minimize losses. If the stock price falls below the strike price, the buyer of the put option has the right to sell the stock at the strike price, while the seller of the put has the obligation to purchase the stock at the strike price, if the holder exercises the option. The owner of the stock gets back his capital even when the asset has a very low value. Investing in stock options is one way to see a more immediate, and often higher, return on your investment than you would see while investing in stocks only.

Owning Defensive Dividend Stocks: *Investing in defensive dividend stocks is one wealth building strategy everyone can use, even when the economy is in a downturn. Defensive dividend stocks are stocks that do not respond to fluctuations that occur in the stock market. This means they continue to generate stable earnings which allow them to continue making dividend distributions no matter the state of the market. Companies that have defensive stocks boast products that are in high demand at every point in the business cycle. It should be noted that defensive stocks are not the same as defense stocks, which are provided by companies that manufacture defense weapons.*

Investing in Hedge Funds: *Due to the risks associated with hedge funds, unless you have a high net worth, it is not recommended for companies or individuals to use this as an investment strategy. A hedge fund draws capital from investors in order to get* *involved in other securities. Because hedge funds are not highly regulated, it is easy and common for them to make risky investments, which can result in huge losses.*

Hedge funds are supposed to reduce risks for investors. However, they also seek to maximize profit. Because they are mildly regulated, hedge funds make use of highly aggressive and risky approaches in order to achieve maximum profit as quickly as possible. This is why you should only invest in hedge funds if you are able to sustain significant losses. The aggressive strategies used by hedge funds only appeal to those who are well endowed since they can afford to lose large amounts of money at one time.

Investing in Private Equity Funds: *Private equity funds often seek more long term investments than hedge funds. They tend to mature over a longer period of time and are managed by private equity firms. Funds which are pulled from investors who engage in this strategy are invested directly in public companies. Private equity funds either purchase small companies, or they buy shares from different companies. One goal of private equity funds is to invest in the growth of a company.*

Similar to hedge funds, private equity funds are made available only to accredited investors, such as pension funds, high-income and high net worth individuals or companies. In some cases, this type of fund is used to buy distressed companies. Private equity funds have exhibited the ability to withstand harsh economic conditions which has drawn the attention of many potential investors over the years.

Gold: Over the years, gold has served as a means of exchange within countries all around the world, even before the use of paper money. Present day, gold has consistently maintained its high value. In fact, those with high reserves of gold stand a better chance of enduring an economic downturn, particularly in those circumstances where paper money begins to lose its value. Armed with this knowledge, individuals and companies that can afford to buy large amounts of gold often do so. It's their way of saving for a rainy day.

You may be asking yourself, "How can I invest in gold?" There are many ways to invest in gold, starting with buying gold jewelry and gold bars. You can also invest in gold coins and gold mining stocks. Buying gold bullion is another effective method for high net worth investors to invest in gold. Some gold stocks pay dividends, and investing in gold also serves as an effective way of diversifying the investment portfolios for many wealthy individuals and companies.

While in the library, I came across several articles involving successful businesses that had lost rights to their brands because they had failed to protect their intellectual property. I marveled at the number of areas in which business owners need to be knowledgeable in order to protect not only their physical assets, but also something they might have created in their minds. I worked around the clock, seeking out professionals who could give me advice on how to avoid the same pitfalls.

TOURNAMENT TIME

March was finally here, and that meant basketball craziness! For college basketball, March was big business. Each year it generates almost a billion dollars in revenue from media rights fees, ticket sales, corporate sponsorships, and television ads anchored around the three-week-long tournament. Despite the lingering recession, experts still projected that our 2009 tournament alone would generate over $600 million in revenue.

I couldn't help but think to myself that this was one heck of a figure for essentially one month of basketball. Black athletes such as myself continuously attract major money and attention to the predominantly white institutions that showcase them. Meanwhile, our black colleges and universities are struggling.

The school newspaper recently wrote an article entitled, "The Jah-Regal Effect: Fans and Money Are Going To Come Wherever the Talent Is." In the article, it talked about how my first year of college basketball at an HBCU far exceeded all expectations. It went on to discuss how my first year single handedly boosted EGC's revenue and endowment and stimulated the local economy. It reminded me and other readers that when our HBCUs are healthy, they bring economic stability to the Black neighborhoods and communities that host them. After reading the article, it was as if everything clicked. At this moment, I finally realized that God brought me here for a bigger purpose, and I intended to prove that I was up for the task.

We went on to win our conference tournament, so that gave us an automatic bid in the National Tournament as the #15 seed. I was so ready to showcase my skills in the National Tournament against the #2 seed. I'd trained hard, kept a healthy diet and lifestyle, and now, it was time for business on the court. The National Tournament was the biggest stage for a college athlete and for me, everyone was watching to see if I would live up to the hype. And boy did I deliver!

It wasn't easy, but we made it to the Final 4. We had to play through many tough teams but my team performed beyond expectations. We lost our final game by 1 point to the #1 seed. It was the only other program that I would have committed to had I not gone to EGC. I ended up setting a tournament triple-double record for points, assists, and steals by a freshman and for any player from an HBCU.

My first collegiate season had played out very well. I had a very decorated first year, receiving the following accolades: making the conference's All-Freshman team, Conference Tournament MVP, Conference MVP, First-team All Conference, First-team All-American, National Freshman of the Year, Final Four Most Outstanding Player and National College Player of the Year. I also made the First National Tournament team. The series of games and practices I had been to with my Dad had finally paid off!

After such a successful freshman year performance, it was practically written for me to go pro, but I decided the pros could wait. Immediately following the National Tournament, I announced that I would be returning for my sophomore year in college. Everyone thought that I was crazy, but I was no stranger to proving myself right and proving people wrong. The National Tournament showed me that we were just one or two pieces away from being championship contenders. Additionally, I'd started to build a solid financial foundation and realized I didn't have to rush. I wanted to take my time and grow my business to its best state before leaving EGC. With the help of Rachel, I purchased a 4-plex near campus to live in and rent out. The income I received from that property made my financial foundation even stronger.

* * * * *

The three years I spent at EGC were amazing for my professional and personal development. I became more confident and stronger as a Black man, gained financial independence, made lifelong friends and mentors, built a network all across the world, and most importantly, I met Rachel, my future wife.

In the two years following my Freshman year, three other top ten D-1 recruits committed to EGC, and we were able to form the first ever "HBCU Big 4." During my Junior year, we led EGC to its first ever National Championship. After that, I decided to leave for the pros after my Junior season and went second overall in the draft to the New Orleans Lions. This was the first time, since Earl Monroe, that an HBCU player was drafted this high.

I was blessed that my Grandparents, especially Grandma Lindsey, my Dad, my Mom, and others had instilled so much positivity and financial acumen in me. I watched a lot of my peers struggle with tuition, room and board, and student loan debt. I was fortunate not to have those problems, not because everything was paid for me, but because I was taught how to "do for self" and build my own wealth. Every lesson I learned in and out of the classrooms in college, prepared me to be the leader and businessman I had become.

After two years of being in operation, I decided to turn my food truck business, "Your Wingman," into a franchise. And now, it essentially runs and pays for itself. I was able to secure contracts with several HBCUs and PWIs, and now, "Your Wingman" is a local food establishment on college campuses across the nation! Those contracts were a HUGE asset in building my wealth portfolio.

Rachel and I started out as friends, but eventually, we started dating. She hasn't left my side ever since. I've always admired the fact that she had her own drive for success and wealth apart from me, but we were also able to build together. In some ways, we're the business power couple version of Dwayne and Whitley. We eventually ended up getting married after we both finished college. During my rookie season of playing pro basketball, I took online courses to help me finish school on time. As I reflect back on my time at an HBCU so long ago, I can't help but appreciate not only the lessons my parents and grandparents taught me, but also the experiences I was fortunate enough to share with them..

A few years later, as I was replacing the old picture frame of my high school homecoming picture of my Grandma Lindsey, my Granddad and I on the football field, and I found a folded, handwritten note to me from my Grandma Lindsey that read:

My Dearest Jah-Regal aka "God of Kings",
I am not sure when or if you'll ever see this
note. If so, I pray it's not too late and that
you'll truly understand what I have been
trying to teach you since you were a kid. Your
generation is the key! If you don't remember
anything else, remember that we need our
Black institutions (i.e., our families, churches,
community organizations, banks and
especially HBCUs) to create stronger Black
economic development and
entrepreneurship. Only then will we see
significant shifts in our income, wealth,

home ownership, business creation, jobs and political power!

Never forget me and never forget that the goal is to always strive to push the family, community and culture forward!

I'm so very proud of you!

Love,

Grandma Lindsey

ROI ON HBCUS: THE ROLE OF HISTORICALLY BLACK COLLEGES IN THE 21ST CENTURY

WRITTEN BY
MARCUS NOEL

In Mrs. McKeever's third grade class, I remember reciting one of Malcolm X's famous quotes: "We didn't land on Plymouth Rock, Plymouth Rock landed on us!" I'm not sure anybody in my classroom had an idea what he was talking about, not even Mrs. McKeever.

As a culturally-exposed black student, I had a question: *How could I become fully educated if the history books and curriculum presents only one perspective of the world?* My answer was to choose to attend Morehouse College in Atlanta, GA.

Eight years after graduation, this February I had the opportunity to speak at a White House panel celebrating

Historically Black Colleges and Universities (HBCUs). But it was not without its soul-searching: What is so special about the HBCU experience? Why turn down Ivies and other top ranked institutions for HBCUs? Why don't HBCU alum give back like other alumni? What purpose do HBCUs serve today?

AN OVERVIEW

HBCUs were created in the mid-1800s during segregation—a time when racism was explicit and educating students of color was neither a priority nor encouraged. Since that time, HBCUs have played a pivotal role in transforming the landscape of higher education in the U.S. Today, there are 100 HBCUs in 19 states plus D.C. and the Caribbean and enrollment stands at over 300,000.

Things could be going better. HBCU attendance by black students has fallen from 18% in 1976 to 8% in 2013. Schools are under-funded (more than half of HBCUs are public institutions) with low endowments and tepid support from private donors, including alumni. Students are experiencing increased student/family debt and depressed graduation rates, mainly due to financial pressures. But their core challenges are tightly related to access to capital and quality of resources, not a lack of talent, ability or intellectual prowess of its students or faculty.

Just 22% of black young adults had a bachelor's or higher degree in 2014 compared with 61% of Asians and

41% of whites (15% for Hispanics and 31% for two or more races). The rebound of HBCUs may be the single most important fix to the educational attainment gap and its wide ripple effect in the economy and lives of black and all Americans. Here's how.

VALUE PROPOSITION

The value is in the experience. HBCUs are diverse and differentiated by their unique culture. They are *experts* in educating and creating opportunities for black people. They also serve as a place of learning for students of all races open to understanding the "black experience;" in 2013, non-black students made up 20% of HBCU enrollment. More than just academic environments, HBCUs are communities. Cultural identity, a lift-as-I-climb spirit, a culture of altruism and a commitment to achieve excellence are all at the heart of an HBCU education.

They are rare institutions where individuals of the Black diaspora can unapologetically take risks, learn and thrive without having to engage in "Double Consciousness" (see "The Souls of Black Folk" by W.E.B. Dubois) or the pressures of being a minority in a predominantly white institution (PWI). Let's revisit Malcolm X:

It is imperative that black people first learn amongst their own communities, then after gaining a thorough knowledge of ourselves, our own kind, and racial dignity has been instilled in us. We can then pursue any school or endeavor and still retain our race pride, racial dignity and be able to avoid the subservient inferiority complexes that most blacks experience in integrated environments.

For more than a century, HBCUs have graduated countless leaders in their respective fields. A short list includes Dr. Martin Luther King Jr. (Morehouse College), Oprah Winfrey (attended Tennessee State University), Marian Wright Edelman (Spelman College), Thurgood Marshall (Lincoln University/Howard Law), Jerry Rice (Mississippi Valley State), Samuel L. Jackson (Morehouse College), Common (Florida A&M University), Toni Morrison (Howard University), and The Tuskegee Airmen (Tuskegee University).

According to an U.S. Commission On Civil Rights report, HBCUs are credited with creating the American black middle class. The report states that HBCUs have produced 40% of African-American members of Congress, 40% of engineers, 50% professors at PWIs, 50% lawyers, and 80% of judges. The impact of millennial HBCU alum are found across all industries: Wall Street, Capitol Hill, Hollywood, on campuses like Harvard Business School, Johns Hopkins, Stanford GSB, at companies such as McKinsey, Goldman Sachs, Google, Apple -- and even on Forbes' 30 Under 30 lists.

This year Prince Adubu, a Morehouse College senior, was selected to represent Zimbabwe in the International Rhodes Scholar Class of 2016. Abudu is the fourth Morehouse student to be selected for the prestigious scholarship at the University of Oxford in

England, where he will pursue a MS in computer science and an MBA.

COMPETITIVE LANDSCAPE

Let's discuss the issues that aren't accounted for when those annual "college rankings" drop. There are several that negatively impact HBCUs, such as generational pedigree, brand recognition, access to resources and exposure and endowment giving. Top-ranked institutions like Harvard University and Williams College were founded in 1636 and 1793, respectively, while most HBCUs were chartered between the Civil War and the Civil Rights Act of 1964. The key thing to know about minting a gold-star academic reputation is that it's cemented over time and fiercely protected from newcomers and diversity.

Endowments are also critical. These gifts help support professorships, scholarships, graduate fellowships and programmatic activities in the institution. According to the Atlanta Journal Constitution, the top 10 HBCU endowments range from $38 million to $586 million, while the top 10 PWI endowments range from $6 billion to $32 billion. A stark comparison. The endowment gap between institutions has doubled in the last 20 years. Another challenge is the rise of college costs over recent years, forcing households to take on significant debt to send students to college.

Currently, 75% of students at HBCUs rely on Pell Grants and nearly 13% rely on PLUS Loans to meet their college expenses. Unfortunately, the black alumni base does not have the wealth capacity to "save" HBCUs. The average black family holds about $7,113 in net worth, more than $100,000 less than the typical white family and a mere 6 cents for every dollar of wealth held by the average white family. Hence, as long as the dramatic racial wealth gap persists, enhanced black alumni-giving will not solve the HBCU financial crisis.

THE SOLUTION

A purposeful and intentional investment in innovation can change the trajectory of HBCUs and their students. From inception, HBCUs were created out of great social need, and while great social need still persists, today's challenges are different. Today, HBCUs have a great opportunity to redesign the institutions for 21st century sustainability yielding long-term positive outcomes. HBCUs have a huge opportunity to be "catalysts for innovation." HBCUs should invest in five key areas: project based learning (PBL), entrepreneurship, social innovation, STE(A)M, and economic empowerment.

A paradigm shift can assist HBCUs to remedy the rampant technology diversity gap where companies have little as 1% employees of color. Every HBCU needs a center for innovation where students can conduct self-led research, develop products, invent, and test their ideas. This will attract both industry and innovative ecosystems to these institutions. As a result, it will create a talented workforce with the mindset of creation rather than consumption.

"GO-TO MARKET" STRATEGY

Adopt Project Based Learning (PBL). *Research shows that PBL is the best pedagogical approach to engage students of color. PBL connects students and institutions with communities and the real world. It gives students the opportunity to leverage technology to solve real problems and address real issues.*

Invest in Entrepreneurship Curriculum. Nearly 75% of students graduating high school say that they are interested in starting a company or working for a startup. HBCUs can leverage this as a training ground for the next generation of innovators of color. Developing curriculum for both entrepreneurs and potential venture investors will help diversify the entrepreneurial ecosystem and allow students to show their skill sets through applied learning.

Build a Pipeline to Social Innovation. *At the heart of HBCUs is community. There is a great opportunity for students to use classroom learning to solve real world problems to potentially impact the world at scale. Partnerships with organizations such as Camelback Ventures, Echoing Green, Global Good Fund, Ashoka, Bill and Melinda Gates Foundation, and Clinton Global Initiative to build a pipeline of talent for the social innovation space.*

Integrate STE(A)M. *Deepen investments in science, technology, engineering, and math with integrated art. STEAM fields are critical when it comes to driving innovation. There are roughly 2.4 million unfilled STEAM jobs in the most influential companies; this number is only growing. Nationally, only 10% of college students are landing STEAM jobs upon graduation.*

Teach Economic Empowerment. *Knowledge alone isn't enough to escape the racial wealth gap. Investments in creating and growing financial sustainability is critical. This will help mitigate the financial pressures and position students and alumni to contribute to endowments and create generational wealth. A deep investment here is mutually beneficial to the community at large.*

DIVERSITY AS THE NEW METRIC OF SUCCESS

Let's leverage HBCUs for what they are good at and *invest* to make them great for the 21st century. HBCUs are the by-product of social innovation. As we become more sophisticated in understanding diversity and the role it plays in educational experiences, we should support the adoption of a new metric system supporting the HBCU experience. This will help express the intrinsic value and power of these institutions.

VALUE OF AN HBCU EXPERIENCE: PRICELESS

For me, HBCUs are priceless. Experiences when Rev. Norris taught (I mean preached) us the "Backdoor Method" of solving complex math equations, Dr. Hollingworth's (a white professor) ensuring that the business and econ majors all had high-quality jobs and opportunities upon graduation. It was also priceless when Henry Goodgame (the Godfather), personally replaced my lost cap and gown on graduation day. Simply put, it was the "village," and that village is *priceless*.

When we look at our ancestral history, our progress and our resilient desire to academically achieve excellence despite the odds, it is fuel for our fire to improve future generations and to establish legacy. HBCUs will continue to be beacons of light not only for the black community but for all of us.

153

Mr.Jamerus Payton

Photo credit: LaTisha Pippen

ABOUT THE AUTHOR

Mr. Jamerus Payton has a diverse portfolio of unique experiences across various cultures and socioeconomic backgrounds. He has combined over 15+ years as a nationally and internationally recognized Serial Social Entrepreneur, Coach, Consultant, Speaker and Best Selling Author.

Mr. Payton, the Co-Owner of Carolina Chicken & Waffles, LLC and Founder of The Payton Insurance Group, LLC, continues to heavily work with and advocate for the creation and sustainability of Black businesses, jobs and investors. Additionally, he is a major advocate for Historically Black Colleges and Universities (HBCUs). His love for HBCUs, technology and community building has led to the creation of HBCU Wall Street. He is also Co-Founder of Code Noir Institute, Inc., an organization that inspires underprivileged youth by teaching technical skills, promoting job creation through entrepreneurship, and produces a pipeline of the next generation of diverse, highly-skilled, STEM-trained professionals and leaders by providing mentoring and career and business opportunities.

Mr. Payton has founded and served on various non-profit boards, committees and advisory boards including My Brother's Keeper (MBK) of Wake County and United Way. He has also served as an advisory board member for the Department of Applied Engineering Technology in the College of Science and Technology at North Carolina Agricultural & Technical State University. Currently, he is a board member of Future Endeavors Life Program (F.E.L.P), a Fayetteville, NC nonprofit that has a vision of helping and preparing underserved and at-risk youth for a future of success.

Mr. Payton has been featured in local and national news outlets such as Black Enterprise, NBC Blk (Black), Blavity, The Washington Post, American Banker and the national television series "Power 2 The People" on The Word Network and The Karen Hunter Show on SiriusXM. He will also be featured in the documentary film, "The Melanin Code". Mr. Payton was also a recurring guest on WCCG 104.5 FM in Fayetteville, NC, where he provided the weekly "Words of Wisdom."

His work has provided him with opportunities to work with Forbes, the UNCF/Koch Scholars Summit as a Business Coach and speak at Entrepreneurship and Economic conferences for major organizations such as the Rainbow PUSH Wall Street Project Economic Summit and institutions of higher education including Shaw University, North Carolina Central University, St. Augustine's University and North Carolina A&T State University. Mr. Payton is also the Co-Author of "Dream Big. Dream Often. Dream Unrealistic. Guidelines To Get

Off The Sidelines," a contributing Author for The HBCU Experience Anthology: The North Carolina A&T University Edition, and the Author of the highly anticipated book, HBCUNomics: A Story Of The Power Of Black College Students, Economic Self-Sufficiency and Financial Freedom.

Mr. Payton is a proud, 2-time graduate of North Carolina Agricultural & Technical State University in Greensboro, NC, where he double majored in Electronics and Computer Technology, B.S. and Manufacturing Systems, B.S. He also has a Master of Science in Management from Southern Methodist University (SMU) in Dallas, TX. He is a 2010 SMU Cox Distinguished Business Leader, a 2017 Washington, DC The Made Man (TMM) Honoree and also a graduate of United Way's Leadership Development Program. In 2018, he was a member of the George Kaiser Family Foundation (GKFF) Dream Tulsa Cohort, a Black Enterprise Modern Man 100 Men of Distinction Honoree, a Black Enterprise Tech Fellow and a Young Alumni Influencer Honoree for The Black Varsity. He is a 2019 North Carolina New Leaders Council Alumni and a 2019 Order of the Living Waters Award recipient from African Diaspora Nation with the endorsement of the African Union.